Monograph 2
AMERICAN ETHNOLOGICAL SOCIETY

MONOGRAPHS OF THE
AMERICAN ETHNOLOGICAL SOCIETY

2

DOROTHY M. SPENCER

DISEASE, RELIGION
AND SOCIETY
IN THE FIJI ISLANDS

UNIVERSITY OF WASHINGTON PRESS

SEATTLE AND LONDON

COPYRIGHT 1941

By Dorothy M. Spencer

Second printing 1966

PRINTED IN U. S. A.

jwc

TABLE OF CONTENTS

This account of the Fijian definitions of disease situations and the relation of these concepts to various other aspects of native culture is based largely on field work which was carried out in the District of Namataku in the Province of Tholo West, one of the Western Hill provinces in the interior of Viti Levu, the largest of the Fiji Islands. For about ten months during 1935–36, with the exception of a short visit to neighboring regions I lived in Nasauthoko, a village in the central part of the District of Namataku.

The problem defined in the present study grew out of a wider range of ethnographical observations made possible by a Pre-Doctoral Field Fellowship of the Social Science Research Council, New York City, to whom I owe the opportunity to visit the Fiji Islands. I also wish to take this occassion to thank Professors Frank G. Speck and A. Irving Hallowell, University of Pennsylvania, for their sustained interest in the project and many helpful suggestions. My gratitude is due to the people of the village of Nasauthoko for their extremely patient and intelligent cooperation while I was attempting to learn their language and studying their modes of thought and behavior. In preparing the Appendix and the data on Pharmacological Therapy, I am indebted for technical aid to Doctor Albert C. Smith, New York Botanical Gardens and Doctor E. D. Merrill, Curator of Botanical Collection, Harvard University, who identified the plants, to Doctor R. A. Lambert, of the Rockefeller Foundation, for supplying information regarding the English equivalents of Fijian diseases and to Doctor F. R. Fosberg, United States Department of Agriculture (Bureau of Plant Industry) for adding notes on the chemical properties of the plants.

Since the Fiji Islands exhibit an amazing diversity, both cultural and linguistic, it is necessary to emphasize the fact that I am dealing, unless it is otherwise specifically stated[1] with customs and

---

[1] I have endeavored to bring together, either in footnotes or in the main body of the paper, all available material from the older sources bearing upon the subject of disease in the Fiji Islands. It is not an easy matter to handle some of the accounts. Many of the older writers do not give exact locations for the customs they describe, but are content to treat Fiji as a cul-

beliefs as they may be studied today in the District of Namataku. There is every reason to suppose that aboriginal conditions with respect to these customs and beliefs, as well as other aspects of native culture, have undergone considerable change in the years which have passed since the first European contacts. These islands were taken over as a Crown Colony by Great Britain in 1874 and the Fijians had come under European influences of various sorts for nearly a century before this time. The first missionaries arrived in 1837 and settled in the Lau Islands from whence they spread over the entire group.

In spite of the fact that in comparison with other parts, especially the coastal regions of Fiji, the inland districts of Viti Levu are relatively untouched, there is no doubt that the aboriginal beliefs and practices regarding disease have undergone profound modification. There have been two main factors at work to bring about this modification. One of these is the Christian influence in the hands largely of Methodist and Catholic missionaries, who have succeeded in converting practically without exception, all of the native inhabitants of the Fiji Islands. In addition to this, the governmental authorities have done their best to abolish especially those aboriginal institutions on the existence of which depended the continuance of beliefs and practices with regard to disease, both by imposing a jail sentence on such individuals who were known to engage in those practices, and by establishing (in 1884) a native medical school in which selected Fijians are given a few years of training in European medical practices and then sent out to the districts to act as doctors for the native population. There are also throughout the islands, in various centers, hospitals with European medical officers, where care and attention is available to Fijians free of charge. In spite of all this, the natives in the region of Namataku at least, still rely to a considerable extent upon their own "medicine men", and rarely avail themselves of their opportunities to benefit by European methods of therapy. Their con-

---

tural whole, and it is somewhat a matter of guesswork as to the particular tribe they have in mind. Allowance has to be made, where statements conflict with my information, for the possibility of change due to European influences. It has seemed wise, due to the fact that these earlier writers had for the most part a long acquaintance with the natives when their culture was still but slightly affected by European contacts, to give their accounts at least the benefit of the doubt, except where ignorance or distortion of the facts is self-evident.

tinued faith in the aboriginal therapeutic practices seems to me to
be due largely to the fact that both the ideas of disease causation
and the methods of healing the sick are so closely interwoven with
so many of the social and religious aspects of culture, that only a
complete acculturation would be sufficient to bring about its de-
struction. It is this interrelation which I have attempted to describe
in the following pages. As a preliminary step, a description of the
relevant features of social organization and an outline of religious
beliefs and practices are necessary, following which a detailed discussion of Fijian concepts of disease and therapeutic practices is
undertaken.

I. Social Organization

Of the various functioning units in Fijian society, the most important social group, for our purpose at any rate, is the *mataŋgali*. This is an exogamous,[1] patrilineal clan organization, the members of which consider themselves to be related by virtue of their descent from one spirit-ancestor, known as the *vu*[2] of the clan. Far back in the past the spirit ancestors of the various *mataŋgali* took wives; and their children became the first human beings.

A vague belief exists in the minds of some individuals that at one time in the distant past all the *vu* of the various clans dwelled together on Nakauvandra, a range of mountains in the northeastern part of Viti Levu, and then later dispersed, each *vu* to the territory he now occupies. One informant expressed the opinion that the dispersal was a result of the great war waged by Ndeŋei, the serpent-god, whose name is familiar to every reader of Fijian mythology, but whose cult was actually restricted to a small part of the island of Viti Levu. Another informant was equally positive, however, that the clan *vu* left the scene long before the war. It was also stated simply that in the days before there were any human beings on earth the *vu* of all the *mataŋgali* divided the land among themselves, and that each lived on his own share; that later they decided to build houses, to beget children and to populate the country.

Regardless of explanatory myths, today each *mataŋgali* is asso-

---

[1] Among those who have discussed the question with reference to this part of Fiji there has been some difference of opinion as to whether or not this group is exogamous. But as far as the district of Namataku is concerned the genealogical material shows that the clan is very definitely exogamous, since out of 174 marriages for which the information is adequate, 161 are exogamous with regard to the clan. In theory it is wrong to marry within the *mataŋgali*, and one informant stated that in the old days persons contracting such a marriage would have been killed. Furthermore, a number of the exceptions to the rule of exogamy may be due to the fact that the informant, asked to give the clan affiliations of distant relatives, gave the tribal affiliations instead. I am not sufficiently familiar with tribe and clan names in the districts beyond Namataku to be able to check them.

[2] The word *vu* means source, origin, beginning, cause; all the spirits that have never been human, those that are not regarded as the spirits of the dead are classed as *vu*, though not by any means all are ancestors of *mataŋgali*.

ciated with a certain territory which it may be said to own; the definite localization of the clan is expressed in the question, "Where is your *matangali?*", rather than "What is your *matangali?*" Land is inalienable and even a clan victorious in war had no claim over the territory of the defeated group. The *vu* of a *matangali* still inhabits his own land and has ever in mind the welfare of his descendants. The ancestral spirit of a certain clan watches over the gardens of his people and if taro is planted carelessly he will come at night and admonish the planter. He is accustomed to inspect the gardens after dark and at such times a light like a lantern may be seen moving about the yam mounds, but no tracks are to be found in the morning. In a small stream which flowed through the territory belonging to another *matangali*, there was a deep pool in which fish could easily be obtained by poisoning the water. Members of this clan before going there to fish made an offering of *yangona*[3] and food to their ancestral spirit asking for his help in the work; and another such offering was made on the bank of the stream. If, while they were pounding the poisonous root pebbles and small stones were thrown at them they knew that the *vu* would help them, but if no such sign was made it was useless to continue the work as they were sure to be unsuccessful. The people of this clan, if they wanted to reserve the fish for their own use made an offering of *yangona* to the *vu* requesting him not to give the fish to members of other *matangali*.

Each village, in which residence is patrilocal, belongs to one clan on whose land it is situated, and the members of that clan are the *i taukei*, the owners, while all other residents in the village are *vunilangi*, strangers, no matter how long they have lived there. An informant would sometimes guess the *matangali* of a certain individual whose village he knew, or locate a clan for me by naming a certain village, but actually members of one clan are not by any means confined to one village, nor is the village entirely occupied by members of the clan on whose land it is situated. This is probably as true of the past, since after defeat in war, refugees often fled to another village where some of them would build houses and settle down, their descendants continuing to reside there for generations. Today a man who has quarreled with

---

[3] The Fijian term for the *Piper methysticum*.

his brother, or who is unable to live down a scandal may take his family and move to another village.

The village of Nasauthoko is occupied by members of seven different *matangali*. The *i taukei* are people of the Matatini clan whose ancestors have lived in Nasauthoko as far back as memory can trace. With their wives they comprise over a third of the population. The rest of the villagers are comparatively new-comers. One man of *matangali* Rewasali, came to Nasauthoko a number of years ago to escape an epidemic of measles which was raging in his own village. He married a woman of Nasauthoko and settled there to bring up his family. Djoseva, whose ancestral home was Vunangoru, a village on the bank of the Sinatoka river, had connections with Nasauthoko which extended back into the past. His paternal grandfather had escaped to Nasauthoko when his village was defeated in war, and there he had remained. His son, Djoseva's father, moved to Wauosi, a short distance from Nasau-thoko and there Djoseva was born. When he was grown to be a young man his clan went to Wauosi and made the necessary ar-rangements to take him back to Vunangoru where he lived for some years. Later as the result of a quarrel with his brother who took a root of *yangona* out of Djoseva's garden without asking permission, he came to Nasauthoko, where he is still living. Semi came to Nasauthoko from Naveauno, a village on the Sinatoka river as the result of some long-since forgotten quarrel with his father's brother. He married a woman from the district and settled down to live in Nasauthoko. Not long before I left the village his young son accidentally wounded a pig belonging to one of the *i taukei*, who in his anger did not hesitate to remind Semi that he and all his family were only *vunilangi* in Nasauthoko, and that they should beware of the wrath of the Matatini men. There was talk after this, between Semi and his wife, of returning to Naveauno after the yam crop was dug.

The clan functions not only in respect to land-ownership. From the standpoint of the individual the members of his group as a whole play an important role from birth to death. It is not the family as such but the clan that is responsible for carrying out the numerous ceremonies which attend the birth of a child. The adult males of the *matangali* are not only in charge of the betrothal and marriage arrangements but may also impose their wishes on the individual in his selection of a spouse. Finally in the series of funeral ceremonies the clan functions as a whole.

The clan organization is characterized by a species of "totem-ism". In the northern districts of Tholo West each *mataŋgali* has as its *i thavu*⁴ one or more plants, and in the case of one clan, an insect. One *mataŋgali*, for example has as its *i thavu* a poisonous variety of yam as well as an insect called *na kurua*; another the *mbua* tree (Fagraea Berteriana); another a certain variety of plaintain. There seems to be no restriction on the use of an edible *i thavu* as food by members of the *mataŋgali*, nor are the scented flowers of the *mbua*, worn ornamentally, forbidden to the clan which claims the *mbua* as its *i thavu*.⁵

In this region of Viti Levu each clan is further divided into a number of named sub-groups, the term for which is *mbito*. It is said that when the *vu* of the *mataŋgali* married, his children became the founders of these sub-divisions, in which descent is also patri-lineal. From the *mbito* headed by the oldest son, the chief of the clan is chosen, who is called the *turaŋa ni mataŋgali*. Though today there is still an individual in each clan with this title, his duties

---

⁴ With reference to the meaning of this word Hocart's remarks (1) p. 445 may be mentioned. He says that the proper term is *vutiyatha* in the west, *idhavu ni yatha* in the east, and that both mean the utterance of the name. It is peculiar that it is his eastern term which corresponds most closely to the one which I recorded, though I never heard *i thavu* followed by *ni yatha*.

⁵ However, Rivers, whose remarks refer to a region not far to the north speaks of an animal "from which descent is traced and whose flesh is prohibited as food" as being associated with the tribe. He adds, "though the divisions of the tribe often have sacred animals or plants peculiar to themselves in addition to those which are tabu to them as members of the tribe." It is not impossible that the clans of Namataku formerly possessed similar beliefs as Rivers who was in Fiji 25 years ago observed even then that "these restrictions and beliefs belong almost altogether to the past, though I met one or two old men who said they still abstained from the use of animals or plants which were forbidden in the old days." (W. H. R. Rivers (1), p. 136 and cf. (2), vol. 1, p. 264.) Hocart considers these animals "vessels of spirits and ghosts" and reports that they are "found chiefly among the High Fijian coast tribes and to a certain extent among the Low Fijian coast tribes. They occur only sporadically among the hill tribes." (See A. M. Hocart (3), p. 737.) Only one of my informants contributed facts which could be interpreted as relating to this belief in an animal as the vessel of a spirit: the ancestor of his clan, he said, sometimes turns into a shark which has occasionally been seen in the Siŋatoka river; it has never been known to harm anyone. It is tabu for members of this clan to eat sharks or any food cooked in the same pot with it. We may note that this man and his family were the only representatives of his clan in Nasauthoko, having come there a number of years ago from their own village in Ŋgalimare, a district south of Namataku.

and honors are so outweighed by those of government-appointed officials as to be almost non-existent; and it is impossible to obtain satisfactory information on conditions in the past. In addition to this each *mbito* has a leader, but his duties are still more vaguely defined at the present day.

Though it is often impossible to show exact relationships, members of the same *mbito* feel themselves more closely related than those of a *matangali*. Before peace was established men belonging to one clan might have gone to war against each other, but not men of the same *mbito*. Breaches of clan exogamy sometimes occur but marriage within the *mbito* is very strictly prohibited. In the Matatini clan there were two sub-divisions represented in Nasauthoko. A man, his father's brother's son, and another "brother" with whom no relationship could be traced genealogically, who all belonged to one *mbito* lived side by side, their houses in a row on one side of the village; and across the green, men of the other sub-division lived close together. Each *mbito* of the *matangali* has a small house, distinguished from the rectangular dwelling house by its square ground plan, which is also called *mbito*, where the old men of the sub-division sleep.

The largest social unit in aboriginal times was the tribe, consisting of a number of clans grouped together to form the *yavusa*.[6] This is a named, patrilineal group, and a unit dialectically, with a few exceptions which can generally be explained historically.

The theory exists that, among the various clans which compose the *yavusa*, there are degrees of rank, and that one *matangali* ranks highest, from the members of which the chief of the *yavusa* is chosen. However we find no logical extension of the idea observed in regard to the clan organization, whereby the *vu* of all the clans would be considered descendants of one ancestor, the first born among which would head the clan highest in rank. No association

---

[6] HOCART's statement (cf. (3), p. 737) that "Fijians call both [tribe and clan] *matanggali*", is not correct for this part of Viti Levu. He continues, "There is in fact no hard and fast line between them, as a clan increasing in numbers constantly tends to become a tribe or sub-tribe while its houses become clans". This may very well be descriptive of a process which takes place, and it is equally true, at least in modern times, that a small tribe may join a larger *yavusa* as a *matangali*, but there is no confusion in native minds regarding what constitutes a *yavusa*, or the difference between tribe and clan, and they are not referred to by one term.

between the *yavusa* and a sacred object of any sort binding the members together could be discovered.

There was among my informants no agreement as to which of the clans that today form the *yavusa* Nambau of the district of Namataku, is first in rank; and apparently this state of affairs is not due to government interference. I was told that in the old days the *mataŋgali* inhabiting the territory could not agree as to which clan ranked highest and consequently the members of the separate clans respected only their own leaders. When "law and order" were imposed by the British the clans within the *yavusa* were urged to elect a chief for purposes of uniformity. This was done and the chief thus chosen was, during his lifetime accorded all due respect by the members of his tribe. His son, however, a person of very inferior intelligence, who would normally have succeeded his father, has lost what authority his father gained, and is referred to with a definite lack of respect; he has never been formally invested with the chieftainship and the clans are again without central authority.[7]

It may be noted in this connection that chieftainship as the well-developed institution found among coast tribes especially in the eastern part of Viti Levu, was not typical of the hill peoples. A. J. Webb, an early observer, noted this distinction: "In their manners the tribes differ much. Those living in the wooded half of Naviti-levu possess an aristocracy, show very great respect to chiefs, and the latter are severely exacting in matters of etiquette. The people on the other hand living on the Sigatoka river and the grass country of Navosa are more of a democracy and pay less attention to such chiefs as they have . . . nor have the chiefs anything like the same influence."[8] I had opportunity to observe the respect paid to chiefs on several occasions when the chief of Maŋondro, the district north of Namataku was present. When *yaŋgona* was being served the first cup was taken to him; people in the house were careful not to sit above him, i.e. further from the entrance door and at mealtimes the others waited to eat until he had finished.

---

[7] Except for the individual known as *Mbuli*, who is a government-appointed official, not necessarily of high rank in native society. The present Mbuli in the district is a fairly popular man and there is some talk of eventually performing the ceremony to confer the chieftainship upon him, though his clan is not of high rank.

[8] P. 625.

But although he was accorded these courtesies, as far as I could judge from a superficial acquaintance and hearsay he seemed unable to exact respect or demand obedience in other matters.

We have seen that the outstanding characteristic of this Fijian society is it's organization into clans in which descent is patrilineal. There remains to be considered a further type of grouping which, cutting across clan and tribal affiliations divides the members of society into two ranks or rows (*ewatu*) so that each individual is either a *lavo* or a *tako*. None of my informants could give any account of the origin of these groups; it was simply stated that they had existed since the beginning. Descent cannot be said to be either partilineal or matrilineal, since a man and his son never belong to the same group; nor is the group of the mother taken into consideration in determining to which of the two an individual belongs. But if a man is a *tako*, his son is a *lavo* and vice versa; or as it is sometimes stated, a man belongs to the group of his paternal grandfather.

According to theoretic statements of informants, these divisions are today at least, neither exogamous nor endogamous, but genealogical evidence shows that a man often marries a woman of the opposite group. Of 207 marriages for which I have adequate information 121 are between people of opposite groups. At the present time the division into *lavo* and *tako* is of comparatively little importance. Natives specifically stated that the groups were not associated with objects of any sort, though Hocart writes that "The alternate generations are connected with the tribal animals and plants . . . the bamboo was peculiar to the *tako* and the *mhomho* plant to the *lavo*. To the latter also belonged the bat." "My questions always received the same answers, that in entreaty the name of the class and one tribal animal or plant would be used, not that of the individual, thus in Nakorosule: '*Tako, lewatuvakei*' (*tuvakei*, woman: the *tuvakei* is the plant) or simply, '*Tako*, give me some fire'."[9] In response to my questions informants said that during the conventional wailing for the dead the group to which the deceased belonged might be mentioned, by saying, "Ah, a *lavo* has left us", or something of the sort. One old man told me that formerly when the game of darts was still played *lavo* would play

9 HOCART (5), p. 223 et seq.

against *tako*. Brewster mentions the fact that in the circumcision ceremonies at Mboumbudho a sham fight took place between the two groups.[10] This same writer says, " . . . certain magic virtues appertain to this relationship. They can render services to each other which would be of no effect if done for one of their own class or generation . . . [a boy was stung by nettles and one of the natives remarked] I am a *tako*; if you are a *lavo* I can give you leaves which will relieve your pain, but if like myself you are a *tako*, I can do no good."[11]

---

[10] BREWSTER (1), p. 314.
[11] *Op. cit.* p. 314.

II. Religious Beliefs and Practices

The key word to a knowledge of Fijian religious beliefs and
practices is *nitu.* Although this word may be translated as "spirit"
Fijians recognize, broadly speaking, two classes of *nitu*, the spirits
of the dead, distinguished if necessary as *yalo mate*[1] and the spirits
who have never been human. This second class of spirits, having
existed since the beginning are known collectively as the *vu* (see
page 1), though many and perhaps all, have personal names and
individual characteristics. Some of these *vu* are the spirit ancestors
of clans and have been discussed in that connection, but many of
them have no such position. They are all more or less clearly
associated with certain localities, and the myths and tales[2] dealing
with their adventures portray their lives and activities as very
similar to those of human beings. There are both male and female
spirits. Some of them, such as the *lewa vusu ndundu*, small, and
beautiful, fair skinned young girls, always singing, who live near
certain water-falls in the district of Maŋondro, or the *ndramu kai*,
old women with grey skins and long hair, who are occasionally
seen near their lake homes, are of comparatively little importance
to human beings. Others like the *lewatcia kana*, female cannibal
spirits, are a continual source of fear. And whether certain other
spirits are beneficent or maleficent depends upon the behavior of
mortals.

Relations between the *nitu* and mankind are close, and the means
by which the living may communicate with the spirits are various.
Nitu, both the *vu* and the spirits of the dead may *kania*[3] or visit

---

[1] *Yalo* is the spirit or soul of a living person; *mate*, dead.

[2] Two broad categories of story are recognized by the Fijians. *Kwalikwali* are concerned with
the exploits of these spirits in the days when no human beings lived on the island. *Talanoa*,
on the other hand refers to any tale, such as an account of pig-hunting, or of an encounter
between a mortal and a spirit or even to conversation in general; *talanoatakinia* might simply
mean "tell me about it", and a guest is asked to *talanoa* as we would ask strangers for
news.

[3] In one sense the word means to eat or devour or consume and has been so translated in
this connection by others. When it is a question of *eating* in the ordinary sense, one would
say:

9

living persons in their sleep. The following is an account of such a visitation by Kitcioni, who was an eye-witness of the events he related. On this occasion a *tuwawa* came to *kania* a woman of Maŋondro. The *tuwawa*, a group of *vu*, many of whom are spirit-ancestors of clans, frequently punish women who have displeased them in any way, by cohabiting with them. In this instance the woman who was named Vani, was heard muttering and moaning in her sleep. Kitcioni asked her what was the matter but received no answer. Vani's teeth were clenched and he could not force her jaws apart. Bringing a pig spear, he put the point of it into a gap left by a missing tooth and pried her jaws open. He then asked, "Who are you?" and the spirit replied, "I am a *tuwawa*." In the course of the conversation which ensued between Kitcioni and the *nitu*, the *tuwawa* said that he was cohabiting with the woman because she had pulled up a *yaŋgona* root in a place where he had lived. Kitcioni's efforts to force the *tuwawa* to desist were unsuccessful, and he finally had to call in another man, the spirit-ancestor of whose clan was a friend of the *tuwawa*, and he succeeded in persuading the spirit to depart. All spirits do not visit mortals by way of punishing them, however. They may do so to impart information of one sort or another, and it sometimes happens that a spirit will be induced to visit one of the living in order to give information concerning the cause of a person's death. If it is desired to detain for a while the spirit who is visiting an individual, it is only necessary to tie a cord around one of the house posts and the spirit will not be able to free himself.

While dreams are not ordinarily of great importance as means of communication with the *nitu*, *vu* as well as *yalo mate* frequently appear to human beings in visions, *yandra*,[4] sometimes to warn or to give advice. In one instance, Kitcioni in a vision saw his friend, Levani, a man who was still living at the time. It was later learned

---

> *a ŋgei kana na vitua.*
> he and ate the yam

The construction is quite different when a spirit is said to *kania:* *a ŋgei kana elia*
  he and ate a certain

na nitu i vua elia na tuŋgwaŋgwa.
the spirit to him a certain the old man

I have preferred not to use the term "possess" in this connection as informants have agreed that the spirit does not actually enter the body. *Visit* which was the translation given by my interpreter seems to me best to convey the idea of *kania* in this sense.

4 For the difference between dreams and visions see, D. M. SPENCER.

that the *yalo mate* of Levani's dead wife had appeared to Kitcioni disguised as her husband, because her funeral ceremonies had not been properly performed.

A very frequent experience by means of which *nitu* establish contact with the living is known as *vakaumata*. This word seems to contain the idea of disguise; it may be analysed into *kau*, to take, and *mata*, face, and means therefore "to take the face of." A spirit may appear in disguise to an individual in his sleep; or he may accost him while awake, on a path, or perhaps in his garden. *Lewa nitu*, female spirits, frequently appear to men in the guise of beautiful young girls, and Siva's experience with one of them, Lewatu Momo by name, is typical:

In the Methodist Church men are often chosen to go to various villages to preach for one Sunday. A young man named Siva who lived in Nailaŋa, a village in Mba, was chosen to preach in Teindamu and he started out from home on Saturday. As he was walking along the path, he looked behind and saw an old Indian woman following him. They came to a high hill and when he reached the top he saw another Indian woman, not quite as old as the first, walking along in front of him. As he was walking faster he soon passed her, and then, coming to a sharp turn in the path, he saw a third Indian woman. But this one was young and very pretty; she wore long flowing garments, on her arms were many bracelets, and around her forehead was a golden ring; her hair and her face were beautiful, and she was neither too tall nor too short. He passed her too on the way, but as they went up a hill she vanished and Siva saw coming towards him Rimivani, his sweetheart. When they met Siva said to her, "Where have you been, Rimivani?" And she told him that she was on her way home from Lautoka. About this time it was beginning to grow dark and Siva said to her, "Rimivani, we have been sweethearts since we were very young. Now I want to cohabit with you." The woman who was really Lewatu Momo, pretended to be reluctant as Rimivani would have been. "Now listen, Siva," she said, "you are a preacher; you are going to preach tomorrow, you mustn't think of such a thing. But Siva replied, "Why don't you go on then?" But Rimivani continued, "If you do such a thing as this I will be the one to report you to the mission; I will tell them that you cohabited with me." "I don't care," said Siva, thinking that she was only joking, "I won't die if you do report me." Still she would not let him. Finally he said, "Look here, after we do this I will marry you. We have been betrothed for many years. There is no need to report me to the mission; I promise to marry you next week if you let me have intercourse with you." So then she agreed. After they had cohabited the girl vanished, leaving Siva lying helpless, weak and feeble on the ground. He managed to reach Teindamu and to preach on Sunday, but on Monday he returned to his own village. He no sooner reached his house than he fell down dead.

So far we have considered several means by which spirits are able to establish contact with the living. It is also possible for mortals to influence the *nitu* in various ways, to obtain help by means of prayer and ceremonial offerings, and to propitiate maleficent spirits by performing certain rites. Prayers (*na masumasu*) may be made by individuals at any time and as it were, informally. They must however, be accompanied by an offering (*ne i sevusevu*) of *yaŋgona*; *yaŋgona* being, in the words of one informant, "the path to everything", it is impossible to address the spirits except through the medium of *yaŋgona*, though the idea of an offering is also present. On one occasion a man suffering from a slight headache made such an offering and prayer to the *nitu* asking that his pain be relieved. Another man, intending to make a journey to a neighboring village on the following day, in a prayer requested his *luveniwai* spirit[5] to precede him and announced the coming visit so that his future host would have time to prepare for his arrival. It was also a recognized procedure to pray to the *nitu* asking that a certain individual be killed and today it is not uncommon for a respectable church member to ask the Christian God to do away with someone whose presence seems undesirable.

A situation which has resulted from the ill-will of the *nitu* may be improved by performing a ceremony called *i mandrali* to the offended spirit. Of this word Hazlewood says, "An offering to the gods, generally as a thank offering, but not as a sacrifice or atonement";[6] and in Lau the word seems to mean according to Hocart,[7]

---

[5] See below.

[6] Hazlewood I. We are dealing here, it seems obvious, with regional variation in the use of this word. WILLIAMS, p. 181, says "after successful fishing for turtle, or remarkable deliverance from danger in war or at sea, or recovery from sickness, a *madrali*—a kind of thank offering—was sometimes presented."

[7] HOCART (4), p. 189.

"a thanksgiving offering" but whether made to the spirit or to the priest who acts as intermediary between the spirits and the living, is not clear. In any case the word is used in Namataku with a very different meaning. The *i mandrali* is certainly not usually, if ever, made as a thanksgiving ceremony; its main function is clearly to propitiate, but I doubt if the idea of atonement is present. It is frequently resorted to when illness has resulted from offending the *nitu* and later will be discussed in detail in that connection. It is also necessary to make this ceremonial offering on certain other occasions, such as starting on an expedition to procure the stone used in love magic, at which time it is necessary to make the *i mandrali* to the *matangali*, the *vu* of which owns the rock; and in transactions involving a whale's tooth, *tambua*, the most important Fijian valuable, the *i mandrali* should be made to his clan *vu* by the giver who explains that the *tambua* is being transferred to another group; and a second such ceremonial offering is presented to the *vu* of the giver's clan by the one receiving the gift.

The question of ancestor worship in Fiji has received a great deal of attention from the time of Williams down to the present day. Basil Thomson in his article on Ancestor Worship and the Cult of the Dead[8] and A. M. Hocart[9] reduce all Fijian religion to ancestor worship. Hocart, who had some acquaintance with the area with which we are concerned, writes of the religious beliefs of the "highlanders" in general, "There is . . . a countless host of beings who are said to be neither ghosts of the dead nor ancestors; they are known as *kalou rere* in the East; the West calls them *uluvatu* (stone heads), and groups them together with *tuwawa*, *ndrim'*, *mandingi*, and others, as distinct from the *nitu* proper. But the cult is not materially different from that of ordinary ghosts. . . .

"In the Highlands and the west, they are spirits of war. . . . It is . . . a reasonable hypothesis that the *kalou rere* was a cult of the dead, somewhere in the Highlands, which so struck the imagination, that it spread all over, and of course no tribe but the

---

[8] Cf. his article in HASTING's Encyclopedia of Religion and Ethics, on this subject, under Ancestor Worship.

[9] Cf. especially his article on The Meaning of *Kalou* and the Origin of Fijian Temples.

inventor would know who the spirits really were."[10] Brewster, whose work on the hill tribes deals with the customs and beliefs of the interior peoples among whom are to be numbered the natives of Namataku, writes: "Their old religion was that of ancestor worship. . . . The first known progenitor was styled the *Kalou vu* or originating spirit, and was worshipped as the tutelary genius of his people. At his death, he passed into the realms of the gods and watched over and protected his descendants, whilst his spirit entered his successor who became his shrine in this world, his reincarnation. . . . In times of sickness, drought or the contrary, sacrifices and offerings were made . . . to the family heads as propitiations to the ancestral spirits."[11] This author is obviously considering the attention paid to the spirit-ancestor of the clans, the *vu*, to which reference has already been made, synonymous with ancestor worship. At the present time, at least in Namataku, there is no evidence that would warrant any statement that the spirit part of the *vu* "entered his successor who became his shrine in this world. . .". Death and subsequent passage into the "realms of the gods" are facts which are not exactly compatible with the beliefs held by our natives regarding the nature of the *vu*.

Whether or not we have here another instance of the amazing diversity of custom and belief characteristic of Fijian culture throughout, or whether it is merely a question of change due to acculturation, cannot now be decided. At any rate it would not be wise to lump the Fijians of the region of Namataku with other ancestor-worshippers, without at least a few qualifying remarks.

As to whether or not in Namataku, spirits of the dead, as well as *vu* have prayers and offerings made to them, I have no instance of prayer addressed to any but *vu*; and though I neglected to ask specifically concerning this point, I think it unlikely that it is

---

[10] *Op. cit.* p. 446. These are somehow equated with the *luveniwai* which is, according to HOCART the modern name for them. HOCART concludes his paper with the following remarks, "Nor will this paper be entirely wasted, if it can convey a hint, which I have so far missed in literature on Fiji, of the diversity which exists . . . even in the very type of religious beliefs prevailing in various regions." In spite of this awareness, he treats the "Highlanders" as a whole, with no concern for the regional variations. The natives among whom I worked had no associations with the term *uluvatu*, and the *ndrim'* are regionally connected with the province of Nandi, and known only indirectly in Namataku.

[11] BREWSTER (2), p. 69.

the custom to pray to the spirits of the dead, since they have no favors to confer or withhold, and since offenses against them are punished by the *vu* of their clans. With respect to the *i mandrali*, one ambiguous statement only suggests that the spirits of the dead might be the recipients of such ceremonies. In response to a question concerning the recipient of a certain *i mandrali* he had made, one very good informant admitted that he did not know whether it had been made to his clan *vu*, or to some of the long dead, human ancestors. It is possible, of course, that such a state of uncertainty is due to the decay of ancient customs, along with the partial assimilation of Christian beliefs.

On the whole the spirits of the dead are not of preponderate importance in the religion of Namataku at the present time, at least. However, a series of funeral ceremonies of great social and economic as well as of religious significance, is held in honor of the dead. Beginning with the night of the burial and successively on the fifth, tenth and hundredth nights following, feasts are made, the series terminating in the *mburua*, the last and most elaborate ceremony which is usually made two or three years after the death of the individual. After this there are no more observances in his honor, but his *yalo mate* continues to be of importance as long as his name is remembered. *Yalo mate* of the long-since dead whose names and individual characteristics have been forgotten have little importance for the living, and they become indistinguishable in a large group of *nitu* concerning the members of which there would be question or argument as to whether one was dealing with a spirit of the dead or with a spirit which had never been human.

In addition to such temporary and casual relationships, the nature of which varies with the circumstance, between spirits and the living, according to Fijian belief it is possible for a mortal to have an intimate and continuous association with one or more *nitu*. In the region of Namataku at the present time, such a relationship is possible only with the spirits who have never been human,[12] and only with certain classes of these *nitu*. Some general

---

[12] It was otherwise in the Lau Islands. HOCART (4), p. 188, says, "Formerly a man's relative would enter him and be embodied in him. . . . Of old, a man at his death became the god of his son, his soul was the god of his son. . . . Formerly feasts and many things were offered as supplications to the souls of men. If a man were ill, a feast would be offered. . . . Then prayers would be made over it, and the name of the father uttered."

features characteristic of all such associations may be noted: One enters upon a personal relationship with a *nitu* in order to procure for oneself certain abilities and special skills which the *nitu* are able to confer; an individual acquires his spirit either voluntarily, from another individual who possesses a spirit, or involuntarily as for example if a man dies without making arrangements to sever the connection with his *nitu*, the *nitu* will attach himself to one of his relatives; in return for powers of various sorts which result from the association, the *nitu* must be "served", given occasional libations of *yaŋgona* etc. Finally when it is desired to terminate the connection a ceremonial offering must be made to the spirit to send him away.

As might be expected, the beliefs regarding the exact nature of this relationship between a mortal and his *nitu*-helper, are by no means definite. The *nitu* is said to stay or abide (*no*) with the living individual, but not to reside within the body.[13] A *nitu* does not, apparently, accompany his human associate continually, but is quickly and easily summoned if his presence is required.

An example of one who exercises extra-ordinary powers by virtue of his relationship with a *nitu*, is the *ndau ni vuthu*, maker of songs, and it is impossible to compose songs without this spiritual assistance. The priest-seer, likewise is powerless without his *nitu*. The individual who, aided by his *nitu*, concerns himself with the curative branch of medicine will be discussed in detail in connection with the treatment of disease.

This idea that persons by allying themselves with the *nitu* can obtain for their own use powers of a super-ordinary nature, is also at the base of all the religious cults for which I was able to collect any information. At certain times spirits belonging to one class have become the objects of organized worship; individuals who "serve" spirits of the same class joined together in a society with common ends and an established ritual. Judging from evidence afforded by such accounts as can be obtained at the present day, it seems likely that at a certain time and in a certain locality a cult directed to one class of spirits predominated to the exclusion of the others. At any rate in the recent past, in Namataku and sur-

---

[13] It may be noted in this connection that the *yalo*, spirit or soul is not thought of as being inside the body.

rounding areas, spirits called the *luveniwai* were the objects of a cult which had become popular in fairly recent times, the last of a series, for the other members of which only a few vague fragments of hearsay could be offered by way of information.

In spite of active interference on the part of the government, until the last four or five years members of the cult continued to "serve" the spirits, and it is still possible to obtain a fairly complete account of the activities which centered around the *luveniwai*. The words may be translated literally as "the children of water," and spirits of this name are found all over Fiji. Generally speaking, however, they seem to play a very different role in religious life elsewhere in Fiji. De Marzan, whose remarks refer probably to Eastern Viti Levu, mentions a *luveniwai* society in his article on Fijian secret societies. "Elle n'a qu'un seul but," he says, "c'est celui d'apprendre des metres ou airs de danse nouveaux."[14] In the Lau Islands where ceremonies connected with the *luveniwai* were held at "festivals for pleasure," Hocart, who refers to these spirits as elves, says of them, "The Children of Water do not live inland but on the shore; they are worshipped only on shores where there is a nice beach. They appear as small men, and do not enter animals. It is said they and the spirits proper are enemies."[15] According to beliefs held by the Fijians in Namataku, however, the *luveniwai* have no connection with water and no explanation can be given to account for their name. They are thought to dwell in a number of spirit villages on the mountain range of Nakauvandra in Northeastern Viti Levu. Among the members of the cult, each of whom "serves" one of the *luveniwai*, is a leader who acts as director of the ceremonies and to whom it is necessary to apply in order to obtain a spirit. As far as can be determined at this period, nearly all adult men, and many of the women who played a subordinate role, were members of the cult. The services required by the spirits seem to have varied slightly with individual cases but generally speaking it was necessary to make a daily offering, called *ne i sevusevu*, of *yaŋgona* to the spirit; some individuals were required to set aside portions of food before eating, and before bathing, to throw a pebble into the stream so that the spirit

---

[14] DE MARZAN (2), p. 727.
[15] HOCART (4), p. 202.

could bathe first. The *luveniwai* spirits for their part were at the beck and call of their human associates, who by means of the power given them by the spirits were able to perform miraculous works and to obtain material benefits of various sorts.

Before concluding this sketch of religious practices brief mention must be made of the so-called "*nanga*" rites, which have been described by Fison,[16] Joske, and others. Although according to the maps of these authors the area of the *nanga* cult included the northern districts of Tholo West, it is not certain, I believe, over how large a territory the rites as they have been described were practiced.[17] However, the chief feature of the *nanga* rites seems to have been ancestor worship. The principal ceremony which took place every two or three years, lasting for seven or eight days, was the occasion of initiating the youth of the tribe into the *nanga* cult. Such other rites as we have information on, have to do with sickness and will be discussed in that specific connection.

---

[16] Fison (1).

[17] Without going into matter in detail, in may be said that the *mbaki*, another name for these rites, was mentioned by my informants as one of the ancient worships, but the few scraps of information they were able to supply indicate that there was very little resemblance to the *nanga* rites of Fison and others. Of course, even around 1885 when Fison was writing, the cult had died out and it is possible, considering the unreliability of Fijian memories on the whole, that my informants were confused; but it is, I think, equally possible, considering the variation that can be observed in other cults, e.g. the *luveniwai*, within relatively small areas, that the *nanga* rites as we know them from the literature did not form part of the religious practices of the people of Namataku and Northern Tholo West.

III. Theories of Disease Causation

As Rivers has pointed out, "One element of the concept of disease and perhaps the most important is that it includes within its scope the factor of causation. There are usually clear cut ideas concerning the immediate conditions which lead to the appearance of disease . . . By starting from etiology we shall find ourselves led on as naturally to diagnosis and treatment as . . . in our own culture."[1] And in this study of Fijian concepts of disease the subject may be best approached by investigating the causal factors involved in disease situations as defined by the Fijians.

A Fijian in a state of health is said literally to be "living well," *e tholathola vina*, and any departure, temporary or permanent from this condition is termed *mate*, a word which expresses the concept not only of illness, but also of death. As is perhaps to be expected in view of the traditional attitude toward primitive beliefs in general, and Melanesian in particular, and, indeed, in view of the facts, earlier writers who were interested in the matter were led to believe that the Fijian regarded all disease as due to causes other than those they termed "natural". De Marzan expressed the typical viewpoint, "Il faut remarquer, qu'avant l'arrivée des blancs, jamais le Fijien n'avait pu s'imaginer que le mort put provenir de causes naturelles."[2] It is unnecessary here more than to mention the fact that such a diffuse term as "natural" has long been recognized as unsatisfactory and altogether inapplicable in this connection. Certainly to a Fijian, disease resulting from sorcery is quite as "natural" as any other illness. In any case the problem is decidedly not to see in how far primitive concepts of cause may be fitted into our categories of natural and supernatural, but it is rather to attempt to discover what are the Fijian categories of disease and on what basis the grouping is made.

Actually Fijians do distinguish terminologically two categories of disease, and practically, three. One of these includes diseases

---

[1] Rivers (3), p. 7.
[2] de Marzan (3), p. 87.

termed *mate vayaŋo* (diseases of the body) which are regarded as casual conditions resulting from what are considered incidental circumstances. Colds and coughs, which are very common, and cuts and wounds received accidentally are usually *mate vayaŋo*. Boils, scabies, ringworm, and other such common and relatively innocuous disorders are in the majority of cases permitted to come and go with little heed or comment. It is not possible however, to assign a disease to this category on the basis of its nature, for prolongation beyond the normal point, or its continued reappearance, or the unusual severity of the case with resistance to treatment, give rise to the suspicion that a certain disease is not a *mate vayaŋo*. In order to confirm the suspicion it is necessary to consult the *vuniwai*,[3] the expert in such matters. Since even a headache or a toothache might prove to be the result of other than incidental circumstances, in actual practice if a *vuniwai* happens to be present, he is consulted very often for trivial ailments, to be, as it were, on the safe side; and on the other hand in his absence recourse would be had to the usual remedies without much speculation as to whether the disease was in fact a *mate vayaŋo* or not.

The second category distinguished by Fijians groups together diseases termed *mate ni vanua* (diseases of the land). At the present time natives differ somewhat regarding the classification, some informants being of the opinion that diseases resulting from sorcery belong to this category, while other authorities on the subject place them in a separate group; and there is some doubt as to the proper classification of diseases which are due to a failure on the part of members of the *luveniwai* cult properly to serve their spirits; but all agree that this second category comprises diseases caused directly or indirectly by the *vu*. In dealing with the subject it has seemed advisable to me to follow the opinion of the *vuniwai* himself, as authoritative, and therefore to discuss under a separate heading the diseases resulting from sorcery.

Diseases Attributed to the Vu

Mate ni vanua, then, are diseases which are the work of the *vu*. While the *vuniwai* might diagnose any ailment as a *mate ni vanua*, there are certain diseases which never result from incidental

---

[3] The role of the expert in diagnosing diseases and his methods of procedure will be considered later.

circumstances.[4] Among these is a disease, or perhaps better a class of diseases, called *sulua* that affects the head. The patient may be afflicted with a headache or a toothache, which due to its obvious manifestations might be thought by the layman to be merely a *mate vayaŋo*, but which the *vuniwai* would recognize as a *mate ni vanua*. Also in this category are diseases termed *ŋwata* (snake) characterized by a severe attack of fever accompanied by the inability to sleep; *na sau ni vanua*, described as a sort of boil inside of the spine; *mata ni loma*, a boil that swells inward; *waŋgaŋga tu i kete*, literally fever in the stomach, etc. It must be emphasized that although these diseases are never *mate vayaŋo*, their true nature is not recognized even by the *vuniwai* on the grounds of external and obvious symptoms. Furthermore any disease of whatever nature might be caused by the *vu*, and so recognized by the *vuniwai*.

All classes of *vu* are able to inflict disease, but they are not maliciously inclined toward the living without cause, and sickness in many cases is a result of incurring their anger through failure to comply with regulations sanctioned by the *vu*, or by committing offenses of various sorts. Even in a case of illness so light as to be ignored ordinarily, a "guilty conscience" might be sufficient to induce the patient to fulfil his neglected obligations without the advice of a *vuniwai*. One very important element in the theories regarding the *mate ni vanua*, is that not only the offending person himself may be punished by the *vu*, but his children and his children's children for generations may suffer as a consequence, until the *vu* has been appeased.

The clan *vu*, who are especially interested in upholding the established order of things frequently indicate their disapproval by inflicting disease when their human descendants, through negligence, fail to meet requirements and thus call down upon themselves the anger of the *vu*. The *vu* may inflict disease directly, or frequently, they enlist the services of one of the *lewa nitu*, (see pp. 24–25) who then takes the face, usually of a young girl and seduces or attempts to seduce the unfortunate victim, with the result that he becomes ill, and unless the necessary steps are taken, dies. In some cases the *lewa nitu* attains her ends by snatching the

---

[4] They seem however, occasionally to occur as diseases resulting from sorcery.

yalo (spirit) of her victim; and a pair of these female spirits, by name *lewa soro*,[5] who frequent various places along the coast of Viti Levu, carry a net with which to catch the *yalo*, as it wanders about at night, of an individual who has committed an offense against the *vu*.[6]

Lewa nitu sometimes bring about the death of their victims by eating the flesh, leaving only the skin and bones. The disastrous adventure of Eneri resulted in death by such means: This man, who belonged to the village of Nawaiwai in the province of Mba, deserted his wife and children and went away to live in Vambuli. Sometime later, he was on his way to a feast to be held in Nalo-tawa, and passed through the village of Nawaiwai, his old home. As it was nearly nightfall, he decided to spend the night there, and he looked around for a place to sleep. All the houses were deserted, as the villagers had gone on ahead to the feast, so he selected a large *mbito* in which to sleep. When it became dark, he made fires in all the fireplaces. To drive away the loneliness, he talked to himself, asking questions and answering them. Presently he heard a sound of coughing outside the *mbito*, and he called out, "Who is there?" It was Lewatu Momo, one of the female *nitu*, and she replied, "Are you[7] asleep?" Eneri answered, "No, we are still awake." And, pretending to speak to someone in the *mbito*, he said, "Don't go to sleep, you there, it is early yet." Lewatu Momo went inside; she caught hold of his hand, and said nothing for a few minutes, merely stared at him. She was very ugly, with sunken eyes, and withered cheeks; her nose and lower lip protruded, but her upper lip and chin were very short; her hair reached to her hips, and she was very short in stature. After staring at him for a few minutes she ate all his flesh, leaving only the skin and bones, and he died.

---

[5] The name is said to mean the women who go together in a row.

[6] This is clearly what has been termed disease resulting from soul-loss. In this connection it may be noted that if the mother of a small child dies a piece of wood is buried with her, so that she will be deceived and think that she has taken her child with her; otherwise her spirit will attempt to steal the child's *yalo* at night and if successfully, the child will die. For other examples see pages 25, 32. All diseases, even all *mate ni vanua*, are not, however, interpreted as resulting from or involving loss of the *yalo*, even though the permanent separation of the *yalo* and the body is co-incident with death. It is therefore somewhat surprising to say the least, to discover in the table in F. E. CLEMENTS, *Primitive Concepts of Disease*, p. 199 that soul loss is the *only* concept of disease causation noted for Fiji.

[7] She used the plural form of the pronoun.

Although there is some reason to believe that formerly the *mbito*, the small house associated with the sub-division of the *mataŋgali*, played a more important part in social and religious life than is the case today, it is still considered essential for each sub-division to have one of its own, though the chief use is as living and sleeping quarters of the old men. But where the group has dwindled, it may be as a result of the death of most of its members or of their transfer to other villages, so that a *mbito* is not actually needed, it sometimes happens that a sub-division does not build one. Failure to do so, however, may cause the clan *vu* to punish the offenders. In Nasauthoko, the Matatini clan is sub-divided into two groups, Nakorosoi and Vatumakuru. Nakorosoi, which is composed of four adult men and their families, has a *mbito*, where old Marika, the oldest member of the group spends most of his time. The composition of Vatumakuru is quite different. The oldest man of this sub-division left Nasauthoko and went away as a preacher some time ago to a neighboring village; of the three other adult males of Vatumakuru, who are brothers, the eldest has a position in the government and is seldom at home: the other two are young men, and one is still unmarried. Until very recently the men of Vatumakuru had not taken the trouble to build a *mbito*. Then Ruveni, a man belonging to the other sub-division of the clan suddenly became ill and died after a few days; and his disease was discovered by the *vuniwai* to have been caused by the anger of Nitulevu, the *vu* of Matatini. In order to avoid any further ill consequences, Simeli who interestingly enough belonged not to Vatumakuru, but to Nakorosoi, immediately set about building a *mbito* for Vatumakuru. In another instance which came to my attention, a small child was suffering from a disease said to be due to the fact that his father had not built a *mbito* for his sub-division.

One very sure way of arousing the anger of the *vu* is to omit the performance or to carry out improperly, any of the numerous ceremonies which mark such occasions as birth, betrothal, marriage, and death. Illness caused by the *vu* was the result of failure to make the *vavanua*, ceremony of betrothal, in the following case: Semi, a man of Wauosi, and Senitoutou met and fell in love at sight. Although Senitoutou had promised to marry another youth, she and Semi eloped to Nasauthoko and were married there. The girl's clan relatives were furiously angry but the young people disregarded them and went to live in Wauosi. Although it was their duty, Semi's people neglected to make either the betrothal or the marriage ceremonies to Senitoutou's clan. It was not long before Semi and Senitoutou became afflicted with disease, and their trouble was diagnosed by the *vuniwai* as a *mate ni vanua* resulting from the fact that the *vu* of Senitoutou's clan was angry because Semi's people had not made the ceremony of betrothal.

In another case a small child was ill because an important detail in connection with his father's wedding had been overlooked.

Whether or not it is a recent condition there is a tendency on the part of present day Fijians to regard as onerous the necessity of making the series of funeral feasts and especially the *mburua* which does entail considerable labor and expense on the part of the performers. Vaula, a man from Sivikoso, failed to make the *mburua* for his father and the following experience which he related to me was interpreted as a result of his negligence. He started off one day to visit his son Naliva who was working at the time in Mba. On his way he came to a deep pool beside which grew a mango tree. He decided to bathe in the pool and having removed his clothes dived into the water. When he came up to the surface he saw a very pretty young girl sitting on a stone under the mango tree. She resembled Lili, a girl of Mba. But on looking at her more closely he saw that beneath her right eye was a black wart, and that one of her front teeth was missing, and by these signs he recognized Lewatu Momo, one of the *lewa nitu*. "Good-day, grandmother of the children,"[8] he said to her. Then he dressed quickly and hurried away. But when he reached home he felt weak and feeble, and all his strength had gone. After a few minutes his breath left him and he did not know when the people came in and moved him to another house. Sometime later his breath returned, and he came to life again. As soon as he was able he set about discovering the cause of his experience and consequent illness.

Some years after she had had a miscarriage, Lusiana was troubled

---

[8] Vaula's daughter was married to a man from Mba, and all the children of that province call Lewatu Momo "grandmother" because she lives in that region.

with recurrent pains which the *vuniwai* diagnosed as resulting from the fact that she had made no *mburua* for the dead child.

Another case concerns a man who did not wait to marry his wife until the *mburua* for her first husband had been made. Ulaiasi as he was called, a man of Nôikoro, was a member of the *luveniwai* cult and served a spirit named Erau. He was cutting wood one day in Lautoka, with some other men, when suddenly they saw a woman sitting on a fallen log, smoking a cigarette. She had a small basket with some tobacco and matches in it. Presently she called to Ulaiasi to come and have some tobacco, and he went over to her. As he sat down, she let the folds of her *sulu*[9] fall aside, and glancing at her, Ulaiasi saw that her genitals were exposed. He said to her, "Have you some tobacco for me?" She said yes, that she had called him over to smoke with her. But the sight of her genitals excited him and he desired to have intercourse with her. "Can we cohabit?" he asked her, "before we smoke." She replied that they would smoke together first. While they were smoking, he looked at her closely; he saw that she was not a human girl, because her eyes were not quite like those of mortals, her speech was very rapid and she used archaic words and expressions in talking. Then he called to his friends that he was about to die, that the girl was a *lewa nitu* and that he was unable to resist her attractions. But he was hoping that Erau would come to his aid. While he was cohabiting with her a whistle was heard in the bushes, a signal that Erau had appeared. Just when Ulaiasi was nearly through with her, the woman suddenly disappeared. She was taking his *yalo* with her, but Erau snatched it back. Ulaiasi lay on the ground gasping for breath, unaware of what was happening, while Erau and the *lewa nitu* fought over his soul. Two of his friends from Noikoro picked Ulaiasi up and carried him home, still unconscious, since Erau who had finally gained possession of the *yalo* had not yet given it back. The two men prepared a bowl of *yaŋgona* and spoke through it to Erau, saying, "Please restore his *yalo* to Ulaiasi." A short time later Erau came to Ulaiasi and speaking through his mouth, said, "Please bring me some *yaŋgona*." When he had finished drinking he continued,

---

[9] The wrap-around skirt worn by men and women.

"Be careful; be on your guard against this woman, if you are seduced by her again I will not be able to help you." By consulting a *vuniwai* Ulaiasi learned that his experience with the *lewa nitu* was a result of his too hasty marriage.

My inquiries concerning Avorosa, a terribly crippled man of Sivikoso, met with the following explanation: He was born, according to informants, with a sound and straight body, and his father, Ratuatama, was responsible for the illness which left him a cripple. Naliva, the brother of Ratuatama, had in his possession a piece of fine *masi*[10] which he was saving for the *mburua* of his father, and he told the rest of the clan not to dispose of the *masi* as he was saving it for that purpose. When, however, their sister, Salosalo, married, Ratuatama gave the *masi* to her husband's people as part of the wedding gifts. Angered, the *vu* of the clan inflicted Ratuatama's son, Avorosa, with disease.

On certain occasions a ceremonial offering of *yaŋgona*, the *i mandrali*, should be made to the *vu* of the clan. For example when an individual is preparing to absent himself for a period of time from the territory of his *mataŋgali*, he is expected to make the *i mandrali* to the clan *vu*, asking permission to go.[11] Sakiusa, my interpreter, suffered a severe attack of toothache which was said by the *vuniwai* to be due to the fact that the youth had failed to perform this ceremony,[12] when he left his village on the coast to accompany me to Nasauthoko.

Whenever a whale's tooth, or *tambua*, is to be given away, the *i mandrali* should be made to the *vu* of the clan. The idea behind this regulation seems to be that the *vu* must be informed that the *tambua* is being transferred to another group, and communication with the *vu* is possible only through the medium of *yaŋgona* of which the offering is composed. A man from Nalembalemba who was visiting in Nasauthoko fell ill because he had neglected to do this; and according to the *vuniwai*, Salome suffered from pro-

---

[10] Barkcloth.

[11] According to rules of courteous behaviour, it is proper for an individual to ask for permission to depart when he is leaving a company of people however casual.

[12] It was interesting to observe that Sakiusa accepted this explanation without question, although among coastal peoples far fewer of the ancient beliefs and practices survive than is the case with the hill tribes; and in addition Sakiusa had with the exception of the last three years, spent most of his life away at boarding school.

longed pains in the head because her husband, Djosatiki, gave away a *tambua* without making the *i mandrali*.

Old and valued objects of various kinds, regarded as heirlooms should not be allowed to pass out of the family, lest the owners be afflicted with disease. From one of my informants I obtained an ancient club in the head of which were embedded 4 or 5 teeth which had belonged to one of his ancestors. Several weeks after this he sent a messenger to me asking if I would please remove the teeth and return them to him, as he was ill and would not recover unless I did so. However, I was permitted to keep the club. Certain other pieces of clan property must be treated with honor and respect. Valala, one of the Matatini clan became ill because the members of his clan had neglected to make a monthly *i mandrali* to an ancient *yaŋgona* bowl in their possession.

Payment to the host clan or village, usually in the form of a *maŋiti* (a feast) accompanied by valuable articles of various sorts should be made on departure of guests who have been fed and sheltered for any length of time. A certain man whose ancestors long ago had been sheltered by the people of Toŋe without making any return for the hospitality, suffered at the hands of one of the *lewa nitu* as a result. As he was leaving Toŋe one evening at sunset he heard the voice of Lewatu ni Nambua, a female cannibal spirit who lived beside a creek named Naloku, in Mba. He heard her calling to her son, "Yaule, come to me." She told him to guard the house while she went to meet the man who was on his way home from Toŋe, whom she intended to kill. Then she entered a hawk and sat beside the path, waiting until the man came along. When he saw the hawk, he picked up three stones and threw them at the bird, but each time the hawk dodged the stones. When the man continued along his way the hawk flew behind. Suddenly the hawk swooped down and scratched the nape of his neck. He swung his walking stick but missed the bird. He continued on his way with the hawk repeatedly scratching his neck until his flesh was torn by the sharp claws. Then as the sun sank below the horizon the hawk disappeared, leaving behind Lewatu ni Nambua, who had taken the form of a woman, and she chased him as he ran screaming for help. His cries were heard by some people of Nayala who were nearby roasting breadfruit. When he came in sight of them he called out, "Stay where you are, don't

run away when I come even though a *lewa nitu* is following me."
They did as he requested and Lewatu ni Nambua abandoned
the chase. After that he was not able to walk until he discovered
that she had attacked him because of the old negligence of his
ancestors, for which he prepared a feast by way of belated payment to the people of Toṇe.

Frequently disease is attributed vaguely to "the old sins of the
ancestors" which have never been wiped out. Losana, who had
been married to Tevita of Nasauthoko for about two years during
which time she had remained barren, consulted a *vuniwai* and was
told that in the past her husbands ancestors had committed "sins"
which should have been expiated.[13] Equally indefinite were the
transgressions committed by Tcolami's ancestors, because of which
this old man suffered a severe infection in his foot. According to
the *vuniwai* they had "shed too much blood in the old wars."[14]

Illness may be the result of angering a living person, and thus
indirectly the *vu* of his clan; the *vu* are said to "pay attention"
to the feelings and opinions of their human descendants and especially to those of the oldest members of the *mataŋgali*. Such a
disease is said to be a *mate ni vanua* and is, I believe, thought to be
caused ultimately by the *vu*, but the anger of the living person is
definitely said to cause the illness and as will be seen later it is
thought sufficient in such a case to placate the living individual.
Several years ago Nanewaŋga had a miscarriage. Being an abnor-
mally shy woman, and not wishing perhaps, to make a fuss, she
wrapped the foetus in a cloth and threw it in the stream without
telling anyone about it. She was very ill afterwards and admitted
to one of the other women that she had lost her child and disposed of it quietly. When this reached the ears of Tcolami, her
father-in-law, he was very angry because she had concealed the
fact. Some time later when she was suffering from a series of headaches and was repeatedly indisposed (she was pregnant at the
time) she consulted a *vuniwai* and learned that her illness was a
result of Tcolami's anger.

---

[13] It might be worth noting that Tevita, in spite of the fact that his wife's condition was
blamed on *his* ancestors was himself the father of an illegitimate child.

[14] Present day informants know too little of the practices surrounding warfare, but I know
of nothing that would lead to the confirmation of the fact that it was formerly thought necessary to expiate the shedding of blood in war; it seems possible that missionaries introduced
the idea in their attempt to stamp out warfare.

Saula, when I knew him in his old age was a very mild old man, but long ago his quick temper had scattered all his clan and he finally suffered from a disease caused by the anger of the members of his village. In another case the illness of Sitiveni was attributed to the fact that he was perpetually disobedient to his older clan brothers.

That the anger of the individual who has been offended is potentially dangerous is evidenced by the fact that the one who has offended should perform a ceremony of propitiation, called *ne i soro* to the person whom he has wronged. Hazlewood translated the word: "An atonement, or something offered to obtain pardon. To *soro*, to sue for peace, to humble one's self, and present something as an atonement for one's offenses."[15] One method of propitiation is to kiss the foot of the one whose feelings have been wounded; or the guilty individual may cover his head or shoulders with ashes and sue for pardon. Frequently he presents a bowl of *yaŋgona* and a small feast, or other gift to atone for his offense. Failure to perform such a ceremony may result in disease. Lusiana, during the absence of her husband, cohabited with another man of the village and became pregnant. When her husband returned, she presented him with a whale's tooth, and a bowl of *yaŋgona* as an *i soro*. Some twelve or thirteen years later she was troubled with headaches, and the *vuniwai* informed her that in order to recover she must make another offering of food and *yaŋgona* as the first *i soro* had not been sufficient.

Some of the clan *vu* are accustomed to look out for the welfare of their human descendants and to avenge any insults or slights. Nauŋavou, the *vu* of the *mataŋgali* of Vasuikoro, frequently feels it an insult to the clan if a Vasuikoro man who makes the ceremony of betrothal is refused by the girl of his preference.[16] Sailosi, a Vasuikoro man, made the *vavanua* ceremony to a girl from Nasauthoko, who refused him and later accepted a man belonging to the village of Wauosi. She was no sooner married to him than she became afflicted with a shaking disease, she could not walk or move without trembling all over her body.

---

[15] HAZLEWOOD, *op. cit.*

[16] Formerly the clansmen were frequently so incensed by a girl's refusal to marry one of their members that they went to war against the girl's clan; and it was stated generally that a girl who refuses one man and then marries another would very likely become sterile.

All the cases of illness which we have so far discussed have been the results of incurring the anger of the clan *vu*. But other *vu* as well make certain demands upon mortals, and the occurrence of disease is often considered as an indication of an adverse attitude on their part toward offenses of various sorts. Vani (see page 10) was visited by the *tuwawa* because she had offended him by pulling up a root of *yaŋgona* in a place which he inhabited. According to the general statement of one informant, if a man happens to be weeding his *yaŋgona* field and sets aside a plant for his *luveniwai* spirit, and then later forgets and pulls it up for some other purpose, the spirit will see to it that he becomes ill or cuts himself with a knife.

Although the religious practices described to me by informants as characteristic of the cult known as the *mbaki* are not identical or even very similar to those of the *nanga* society as related by Fison, the two have one feature in common: an area set aside and sacred to the spirits worshipped by the members of the cult. According to my information one of the female *nitu*, named Lewa Levu[17] was the spirit to whom the cult was directed, and she punished any trespassing on the sacred ground by inflicting disease upon the offender. And although at the present time very few remember even faintly the days when Lewa Levu was worshipped, the sacred grounds are still pointed out and avoided.[18] Recently a young man named Vetheli cut down a *masi* tree which was growing on a sacred ground. Very soon afterwards he began to tremble and shake, having been afflicted with disease; he roamed about the village all day long and even during the night, tearing off his clothes and talking senselessly until finally he died. Lewa Levu likewise visited with disease an old man Mauthava from Tawaleka, who went to a sacred ground and cut down a tree to be used as a house post. But he was not able to get it home so suddenly did the same shaking disease come upon him. According to informants, his mind, like that of Vetheli was also affected, so that he kept

---

[17] *Lewa*, woman; *levu*, large.

[18] Mr. P. Stoebener, at one time connected with the Catholic Mission in the district of Mbemana, south of Namataku, informed me that on one occasion the priest wanted a tree which was growing on such a sacred spot, and that the Fijians who were nominally Catholics refused to cut it down until it had been sprinkled with holy-water.

saying "bad words" all the time. Nothing could be found to cure him and he, too, died.

Although the cult of the *rere* spirits which antedated that of the *luveniwai* has like the *mbaki* long been a thing of the past, and the *rere* are now of comparatively little importance, even today disease may be attributed to their intervention. Kitcioni, whose father had been a member of the *rere* cult, suffered at one time from a sore throat; it was so bad that he could not speak but had to communicate by making signs. The *vuniwai* informed him that his father had never made any returns to the people who had given him the *rere* spirit; that after his father's death they had talked behind Kitcioni's back, saying among themselves that he should now make some compensation to them; and that the *rere* spirit overheard the gossip, took their part, and caused Kitcioni to become ill.

Many individuals have special obligations to certain of the *vu* who manifest their displeasure by afflicting with disease such unfortunate persons as fail in some way to comply with requirements. We have seen that those who have entered into personal relationships with the *nitu* are obliged to perform various small services in return for benefits received. Judging from the records such acts of service, while small, are somewhat taxing in that it is usually necessary to perform them daily. At any rate in many of the cases for which I was able to obtain information, illness was explained as due to a lapse in matters of this sort. During the recent past while still most of the adult men in this region were members of the *luveniwai* cult, a great many ills were attributed to the *luveniwai* spirits. Three or four men of Nasauthoko, fathers of the present inhabitants died from diseases contracted in this way; shortly after my arrival, Meli, an old man, died, apparently of tuberculosis, a disease visited upon him by his *luveniwai* spirit whom he had neglected to serve properly. Old Saula, in addition to the troubles brought down upon him by his sharp temper, suffered off and on for years and finally became deaf, due to his repeated failures to serve his *luveniwai* spirit. Sometime ago in desperation he made the necessary arrangements to send his spirit back to Nakauvandra, in order to escape the obligations and consequent danger of disease.

An individual who has enjoyed a personal relationship with any of the *nitu* regardless of what class must make the ceremony of *i mandrali* if for any reason he wishes to terminate the association; and if he has died without doing this, his relatives must do it for him. Disease is frequently diagnosed as a consequence of failure to perform this ceremony. A man of Maŋondro who "served" a *luveniwai* spirit died without making the *i mandrali* to send the spirit back to Nakauvandra. His son Isei should have then attended to this matter but neglected to do so. His father's *luveniwai* spirit became angry and enlisted the aid of one of the *lewa nitu* in punishing Isei. She took the face of Milika, Isei's sweetheart and met him one day as he was on the way to his garden. When he stopped to speak with her, she offered him some tobacco which he accepted, and they sat down together to smoke. Presently she snatched his *yalo*, so that he suddenly lost his mind and became crazy like a lunatic. Then she assumed her real form and he saw instead of Milika, his sweetheart, a woman with long hair reaching to her knees; she had a black face with a long nose and a small mouth, her eyes were sunken and she had no eyebrows.

In addition to inflicting disease of their own initiative, the *vu* may act at the instigation of human beings. Also classed as *mate ni vanua*, are diseases caused by the *vu* in answer to prayers of the living. In order to make such a prayer a bowl of *yaŋgona* must first be prepared, and when used for this purpose, the root must be pounded or grated; it is forbidden to chew it.[19] On a certain occasion, it was the purpose of the prayer to induce the *vu* to inflict disease on Kasanita, a girl of Nasauthoko, because she had refused to marry Tunivatu. The prayer was made by his fellow-clansmen to the *vu* of their *mataŋgali*. When the *yaŋgona* was ready, Tunivatu was called in and told to sit down in front of the bowl, which was then picked up and placed on his head by some of the men, while another man addressed the *vu*. By permitting the *yaŋgona* to rest on his head, the most chiefly and the most sacred part of the body, Tunivatu was showing the extreme courtesy to the *vu* in order that he might be disposed to grant the request.

---

[19] Although the government has forbidden the chewing of the root for hygienic reasons, it is still done frequently for ordinary social occasions, as this process is thought to produce a superior beverage, but I am told that according to native custom, chewing was always forbidden in the preparation of *yaŋgona* for ceremonial use.

In any case, the prayer was successful as Kasanita shortly after suffered a *mate ni vanua* and died.

If a member of the *luveniwai* cult wished to kill someone, he would inform the other members at a meeting and if they all agreed, *yaŋgona* would be made, and each would pray to his spirit asking that the victim be made fatally ill. Apparently in every case the *luveniwai* spirit accomplishes this by snatching the *yalo* of his victim.

Today prayers are often made to the Christian God for this purpose. Kitcioni's first wife committed adultery with a man from Vaturu. When Kitcioni heard of this, he told me, he was very angry and decided to take the matter to court. This he did but the magistrate informed him that a woman cannot be punished by the court for this offense. "Very well," said Kitcioni, "if you will not punish her, I will ask God to do so." And he returned home, where he prayed to God to kill her, with the result that she soon fell ill and died. Old Marika one evening caused a considerable disturbance when he was overheard praying in his *mbito* to God, asking him to kill the wife of the native missionary, against whom he was cherishing a private grudge. In this case the only result was that Marika was deprived of his position as preacher by the authorities of the church to whom the matter was taken.

Although as we have seen, diseases termed *mate ni vanua* may result from various types of behaviour, including offenses committed by mortals directly against the *vu*, as well as those originating in situations involving relationships between individuals and their fellow men, and only indirectly implicating the *vu*, all diseases of this class are said, categorically to be due to the anger of the *vu*. It must be emphasized here that illness is not an automatic result of wrongdoing, but its occurrence depends upon an apparently variable emotional reaction of the *vu*, and it is obvious to the Fijian that the *vu* overlook or are willing to ignore a great many transgressions. For this reason it seems to me, the fear of disease does not act as a very powerful deterrent if an individual wishes to procede in a way contrary to prescribed behaviour, nor a very strong incentive to conform. The cases which I have cited are obvious indications of this fact. Furthermore in spite of the fact that illness is very frequently attributed to failure properly to perform the funeral ceremonies, during the time I lived in Nasauthoko, four people died, and for not one of them were the ceremonies carried out completely. That the last rites for Merewai were hastily performed and not even a funeral feast provided, was not surprising since her blindness and great age and consequent uselessness, made her death a matter of little moment, and since she had outlived her husband and children, only distant relatives remained. Djoseva, when old Elai, his brother died, managed to provide a funeral feast, but the "fifth night" and the "tenth night" came and went without the proper observances, though this was so much a matter of comment in the village that Djoseva felt obliged to excuse his conduct on the grounds that he needed his pigs for another future occasion. Ruveni, whose death as a result of failure to build the *mbito*, was previously discussed, fared somewhat better, partly because he belonged to the most populous clan in the village, and partly because he died while still in the prime of life, but even in his ceremonies, important details were omitted.

However, the belief that the *vu*, angered by certain human actions are frequently responsible for illness, affords a satisfactory explanation for the occurrence of disease, and as will be seen later, a means whereby health may be regained.

Disease and Sorcery

The third category of disease distinguished by Fijians on the basis of causal factors comprises illnesses brought about by magical means. Here again the obvious symptoms of the disease are not in themselves sufficient to indicate to the observer that he is not dealing with a *mate vayaŋo* or a *mate ni vanua*.

Terminologically magic and medicine are synonymous. There are according to native theory, two sorts of medicines (*ne i ndrotci*), the medicines of death and the medicines of life. All of the medicines of death are properties used in witchcraft, while those of life include substances used therapeutically,[20] as well as materials employed in magic of various sorts where the purpose is

---

[20] It seems likely that the term *wai ni mate* (water of sickness) at present frequently used for therapeutic substances has been introduced, perhaps by the native medical practitioners, and that *i ndrotci*, still used for "medicine" in an evil sense, was once a more general term in this dialect for all medicine.

not to cause disease or death; for example medicine rubbed on the legs to make them strong for a long journey or a race, and the rock with magical properties, the essential ingredient of love magic.[21] Since we are concerned here with the *i ndrotci* only as a means of causing disease, the medicines of life will be considered later under another heading.

Due no doubt to the attitude regarding such matters which has been taken by the government,[22] it is impossible today to find individuals who are willing to confess to any knowledge of the medicines of death other than such facts as they claim to have rescued from heresay. I am inclined to suspect that as a matter of actuality such practices are more rare than was formerly the case, in spite of the fact that cases of disease attributed to witchcraft are by no means uncommon even at the present time; and I think it possible that none of the Fijians with whom I had personal contact had ever engaged in such practices. At any rate, there exists considerable vagueness in the minds of informants regarding important particulars, and the situation is further complicated by the fact that opinions conflict on several points.

However, certain broad generalities can safely be laid down as the basis for a discussion of the various methods of procedure adopted in making medicine to cause disease. In all cases, for which I have any information whatsoever, vegetable material, usually the leaf of a plant, is used.[23] Each of these medicines of death is owned by one of the *vu*, but whether all or only certain classes of *vu* own medicines is a matter of dispute. The *vuniwai* was of the opinion that all of the medicines of death are owned by the *tuwawa*[24] but other informants while willing to concede that the

---

[21] At the present time at least, in this part of Fiji, magical procedures are resorted to in only a few fields of endeavor. Informants disclaim any knowledge of the use of magic in agriculture, housebuilding, warfare etc., and deny that conditions were different in the past.

[22] BREWSTER (2), p. 233: writes "Early in the day we found out what a disturbing and dangerous doctrine witchcraft was, as it led to fights and reprisals, so much so that a very drastic native regulation was enacted, under which the wizards could be awarded forty lashes and two years hard labor."

[23] Elsewhere in Fiji the term *ndraunikau*, literally "the leaf of a tree" is used for witchcraft in general: the equivalent in the dialect of Namataku, *rau ni kai*, is used for certain magical procedures (see p. 41), but not for witchcraft in general.

[24] That the *tuwawa* have a somewhat sinister character is attested to by the belief that they roam about at night, and that if during their wandering they lean against a coconut palm, that tree ceases to bear fruit.

vuniwai might possibly have "inside information" were firm in insisting that they had never heard such a theory advanced, and still inclined to believe that other classes of *vu* as well, owned medicines. In any case before making magic the *vu* of the medicine used is invoked, through the medium of *yaŋgona*, and a prayer made, asking him to kill or to inflict with disease, the victim of the medicine; and only after this is the *i ndrotci* prepared. It is interesting that informants declare themselves unable to state whether the prayer to the *vu*, or the medicine itself, is the means by which the purpose is accomplished.[25]

All magical procedures to inflict disease or death upon a certain victim are based upon two principles: The first is that discussed by Frazer as "contagious magic," whereby some bodily refuse, or an object which has been in contact with the individual is secured and put together with the medicine in a container, usually of bamboo, with the result that the individual himself, is affected by the power of the medicine. The second principle implies the theory of what may be called direct infection, in that the influence of the *i ndrotci* is considered to be transmissible by diffusion, so that it is necessary only that the essence of the medicine reach the victim in some way. As will be seen later, these two principles may be found expressed in the same method.

It is possible for any individual to *ndrotcia*, or to cause disease by witchcraft, provided that he knows the necessary ingredients. Such a one is called *na ndau ndrondrotci*, literally the "maker of medicine." If an individual wishes to make magic and does not possess knowledge of the proper medicines it is customary for

---

[25] This fact is of additional interest in view of the importance in other regions of Melanesia, of the spell, a set form of words, as such. However, the Fijian prayer, while conventional in form is far removed from a typical Melanesian spell. It is possible that in addition to this prayer, some formula is uttered, which corresponds more closely to what is usually termed a spell, but my inquiries on this point always received a negative answer. BREWSTER (2), pp. 233–234, referring specifically to the peoples of Tholo East, reports, "There are many forms of witchcraft, one of which is called the 'Spell of the Plantain.' In that case a sucker is procured, which is taken to some lonely spot in the forest and planted at night by the light of a full moon. It is put into the ground with many spells and incantations, and with many curses on the victim whom it is to affect. It is clubbed, speared, and knocked about, and as it suffers, so will the person it represents. Nightly it is visited and subjected to further tortures, and as it wilts and dies so will the creature for whom it undergoes the evil treatment." On the other hand BASIL THOMSON (2), p. 163 et seq. makes no mention of the use of spells in his general account of wtchcraft. Regarding the use of magical formulae in placing a tabu on property, see pp. 81–82.

him to take a whale's tooth[26] to the clan or village to which he
is *vasu*, in other words to his mother's brother's people,[27] and
to ask for the *i ndrotci*, and instructions for its use. According to
Thomson's account one skilled in magic practices might be asked
to do the work, and payment was made to him upon the comple-
tion of the task. "When the victim died, the wizard claimed his
reward by attending the funeral with a blackened face, and bold
indeed would be the employer who dared to bilk him. This practice was sometimes abused. Any sudden death being ascribed to
witchcraft, a professional wizard, who was entirely innocent,
would blacken his face at the funeral in the hope that someone
who had an interest in the death would pay him a fee he had
never earned."[28] Thomson does not say definitely in what locality
this was the custom, but as one of his examples deals with a case
which occurred in the district of Mbemana, not far to the south
of Namataku, it is possible, since my accounts contain nothing
of this sort, that the practice was formerly found in Namataku
as well, and that the necessity for greater secrecy in such matters
resulting from governmental interference, was responsible for its
disappearance.

While he is preparing the substance to be used, certain precautions must be observed by the *ndau ndrondrotci* in order that the
influence of the medicine does not react on himself: He avoids for
example, in some cases, touching the leaves with his fingers, or he
is careful not to let his shadow fall upon the *i ndrotci*.[29] After
having accomplished his ends the *ndau ndrondrotci* must make the
i mandrali ceremony to the *vu* who owns the medicine;[30] failure to
do this results in illness. Saiyasi, the most famous sorcerer of

---

[26] A *tambua* is presented as a preface to making any request.

[27] His position with regard to these people ensures that he will be given what he asks for,
and obviates the necessity for any return payment.

[28] THOMSON (2), p. 165.

[29] Mr. Buell Quain tells me that similar precautions are taken in Mbua, the western province of Vanua Levu, where he carried on field work. In that region as well as in Lau (cf.
HOCART (4), p. 175) after the death of the victim, the individual who has made the medicine
must spear the corpse or prick it with a needle so that the evil power of the medicine may
escape, otherwise it will react upon the sorcerer himself. My accounts contain nothing of this
sort, and it is interesting to learn that Mr. Quain was informed by the natives of Mbua that
in Viti Levu, this is no longer done "because the people are becoming educated."

[30] Likewise after obtaining and using the love medicine an *i mandrali* must be made to the
vu who owns it.

recent times in this area, who was known to have killed more than a score of people, neglected to make the *i mandrali* for the *i ndrotci*, and the death of his daughter was attributed to this lapse. Another case in which illness resulted from failure to make such an *i mandrali* may be related in more detail, as the nature of the act provoking the sorcerer to action is of some interest: One night Kavunikoro entered Kitcioni's house and lay down on mats beside the fireplace; shortly after Naulunisau, a man from Noikoro, went in and lay down on the other side of the fire. During the course of the evening Naulunisau reached up and took a stick of firewood from the shelf above their heads, but he neglected to ask permission before doing so and failed to clap his hands afterward.[31] This discourtesy enraged Kavunikoro, but he bided his time and waited until Naulunisau was asleep. Then he took up in a shell out of the ashes of the fire some of the spittle of Naulunisau, put it with some leaves in a bamboo container which he buried in the ground. The next morning Naulunisau died. Kavunikoro, however, did not make the *i mandrali* for this and Kitcioni, his brother's son, contracted an infection in his leg as a result. The necessity of making this ceremony raises an interesting point: if the *i mandrali* is considered as an act of propitiation its performance in such circumstances might seem to indicate that sorcery is regarded as reprehensible even by the *ndau ndrondrotci* himself. This does not seem to be actually the case, however, except where the sorcerer carries his work to extremes; Saiyasi was definitely regarded as a "bad man," and the number of his victims thought to be excessive. But in most of the cases related to me, the sorcerer was thought to act with more or less justification. I think it more likely in this case that the *i mandrali* is made with the idea of payment and perhaps of thanksgiving.

Although the fundamental principles we have discussed may be observed in all sorcery there are various methods of making medicine and each is distinguished by special details of procedure, and probably by the use of a different plant, though since informants could not or would not divulge the name of the leaf (except in one or two cases) it is possible that the same medicine is used in several methods; and each method has its own name. As will be

---

[31] According to Fijian etiquette this was very rude behavior; and even more, an insult to the sanctity of the head of Kavunikoro.

seen informants do not always agree as to what details are associated with a certain label, but differences of opinion are, I think, to be expected in dealing with such an esoteric subject. Furthermore it is not likely that the following account is exhaustive.

According to one method, known as the *siŋa ndua*, (*siŋa*, day; *ndua*, one) so-called because the victim dies the very day *ne i ndrotci* is made, a short reed, about a foot long is rubbed with a certain leaf, and then put in the doorway of his house so that the victim will walk over it, and when he does so the power of the medicine will go into him. The *ndau ndrondrotci* then stations himself in a place where he can keep watch without being observed. After he sees that his aim has been accomplished the sorcerer takes the reed and throws it into a stream where the current is swift, so that the reed is washed clean and all traces of the medicine removed. This is necessary because if the reed were found with the medicine still on it, one of the medicines of life could be rubbed on the reed and the victim cured of the disease. A *ndau ndrondrotci*, named Kurayavaki of Wauosi used this method to kill Manoa, a man belonging to the village of Sivikoso, and Savenatha, of Tambalei. Kurayavaki was already betrothed to Karolaini when Manoa went to her and succeeded in persuading her to marry Savenatha instead of Kuruyavaki. And as his revenge Kuruyavaki resorted to *ne i ndrotci*.

Medicine to cause blindness, termed *ne i ndrotci ni mata* (*mata*, eye), is made simply by placing dried leaves of the proper sort in the fireplace. The victim, when he is about to make a fire, gathers up the medicine with the rubbish to be burned, sets fire to it and is blinded by the smoke. Isoa, of Sivikoso was pointed out as an example of blindness due to such a cause, but no reason for the action of the *ndau ndrondrotci* could be given.

Mbelo is the name given to another method of sorcery. The term is said to refer to the fact that the neck of the individual suffering from the disease thus caused, grows long like the stalk of the *mbelo* plant (?). Informants differ regarding details of this procedure. According to one informant refuse or some object belonging to the victim, together with the leaves, are put in a clay pot and a little water is added. The pot is then placed over the fire, and as the contents become heated, the victim breaks out into a sweat, falls ill and dies. According to another account,

the refuse obtained from the intended victim is put in a bamboo
container with the leaves, and the container is then closed with a
lid and placed in a stream beneath the water. When the lid rots
the essence of the medicine rises to the surface of the water in
bubbles, which, breaking, permit the essence to escape so that
the victim is affected, and becomes ill.

Magic of the type described in this second version was responsible for the death of Tuimba, a man of Nakumbuwai. People of
Talilevu's clan, located in Mbukuya, made the ceremony of
betrothal to a girl in Ŋgalivunda, and after she had accepted
Talilevu, she cohabited with Tuimba. They were discovered in
the act and when the news of her inconstancy reached Talilevu
he was very angry and made the *mbelo* magic against Tuimba.
As a sequel to the tale it may be mentioned that after Tuimba
had died, Talilevu's clan made another ceremony of betrothal to
the girl, but this time she refused and fled to Tambuŋguto, where
she married another man.

The operation termed *vualiku mbalavu* (*vualiku* means north wind
specifically but any wind may be used depending upon the case;
mbalavu, long) is somewhat similar in principle to the second
version of the *mbelo*. The *ndau ndrondrotci* climbs to the top of a
high hill and waits for a wind to blow in the direction towards
which his victim lives. He then holds the bamboo containing the
i ndrotci[32] so that the wind may waft the essence of the medicine
to the victim. The famous, aforementioned Saiyasi by this method
killed a man living far to the south-west, in the province of
Nandroŋa.

Two distinct procedures, both known as *mondroka* receive their
name from the leaf used.[33] According to one method the sorcerer,
using little reed tongs, soaks a piece of tobacco in a cup of water
containing the medicine, and later gives it to the victim who
becomes ill when he smokes it. In the other method of the same
name, the leaves are shredded and put in a bamboo container.
The *ndau ndrondrotci* obtains on the end of a stick some spittle of the

---

[32] Unfortunately I do not know whether in this case refuse from the body of the victim or
an object belonging to him is a necessary ingredient.

[33] Informants knew this leaf by name only; they claimed to be unable to recognize it in
the bush.

individual whom he intends to kill and adds it to the leaves. He then proceeds to dig a hole in the ground in which he buries the bamboo. If he wishes to kill the individual, at the end of several weeks he covers the hole with soil, and on that day the victim dies. A girl in the province of Nandi suffered from a disease caused by this type of *mondroka*, made by the father of a man she had refused to marry. In this case the sorceror did not cover the hole and the *vuniwai* was able to cure her.

Rau ni kai mbalavu ("long leaf" literally; here leaf is used for "medicine") must be made at night. The sorcerer conceals the bamboo containing medicine and some object belonging to his victim, in a lonely place where it will not be found. If he wishes merely to inflict disease he covers the bamboo with a leaf, but if he intends to kill his enemy he closes the mouth of the bamboo tightly with cloth or a piece of wood. The name *rau ni kai mbalavu* refers to the fact that the victim does not die immediately but suffers from the disease off and on for a long period, his skin becomes white and he gradually grows more and more feeble.

According to the procedure termed *rau ni kai thuŋgethuŋge*[34] one of the medicines of death is pressed together with a crumb of the victim's food or bodily refuse of some sort, and mixed with a little water, in a fibrous strainer; it is then put in a bamboo container and hidden in a secret place. This results in instant death, but if the sorceror wishes to prolong for a time the life of his enemy, he adds one of the medicines of life to the ingredients, to cause a lingering illness.

All types of sorcery so far discussed, have been made with a certain definite individual in mind. But magic may also be made with a view to protecting property against possible thieves. Anyone who takes property thus protected becomes afflicted with disease, a sign to all that he has stolen the fruit, and a punishment for his misdeed. One informant supplied the names of two leaves used in placing a tabu on the property: the *tautau* (?) and the *totondro* (*Centella asiatica Uurban*); this second leaf is also, strangely enough, one of the medicines of life. To tabu a tree of any sort, the medicine is buried in the ground at the foot of the tree, or the

---

[34] *Thuŋgethuŋge*, begging, is said to refer to the act of begging the *vu* who owns the medicine to kill the victim.

leaf may be rubbed on a reed and the reed then rubbed against the trunk of the tree. A pole (*na sara*, or *na tambu*[35]) is then planted in the ground beside the tree to show that a tabu has been placed on it. Kitcioni once climbed a coconut palm and took some nuts without noticing that the tree was tabu, and as a result he suffered from an infected toe. Apparently not in every case, however, is notice given to the public that a certain plant has been placed under tabu. Sugar cane, for example, may be tabued by shredding a leaf and placing it on the ground where the cane is growing. A speech is made, in which the leaf is told to guard the cane, and to punish thieves, but according to informants there is no set or prescribed formula for the speech (one old man informed me that in the old days, powerful magicians were able to tabu crops, simply by addressing the garden, without being obliged to use leaves). A certain woman ate some sugar cane which she had stolen, and which had been under a tabu, and her mouth became covered with *varavara*.[36] It was explained to me that in the first example disease centered in the toe because the man had climbed a tree on which the medicine had been rubbed, while in the second, the woman's mouth was infected because she sucked the sugar cane.

Magic may also be made to punish a thief who has stolen property even when no tabu has previously been placed upon it. If a man finds that yams have been stolen from his garden, he may put medicine in the empty yam mounds and as a result the thief will suffer from a swollen arm.

It was noted in connection with the discussion of *mate ni vanua*, that some informants were of the opinion that diseases resulting from sorcery also belonged in that category. There are very good reasons it seems to me why this confusion exists. We have seen that all medicines of death are presided over by the *vu* who in the last analysis are thought to cause the diseases occurring as a consequence of witchcraft, as well as *mate ni vanua*, so that sickness brought about by sorcery is not exclusively a matter of human agency. Furthermore it will be remembered that *mate ni vanua* are not always matters exclusively of spiritual agency; a human individual may pray to the *vu* asking him to inflict illness upon

---

[35] The Fijian equivalent for tabu.

[36] Scabies, an infection so common that it is usually treated as a *mate vayaŋo*.

the enemy, and his action differs from that of the sorceror only in that no medicines are used; and even the sorceror is unable to decide whether the prayer or the medicine is the more powerful in bringing about his ends. When we come to the problem of diagnosis and treatment it will become apparent that in this aspect of disease also, no line can be drawn between *mate ni vanua* and diseases resulting from sorcery.

A species of sorcery of another type, not strictly comparable with any we have so far discussed, has been described by an early student of Fijian customs and beliefs, Dr. B. S. Corney, who for many years was the chief medical officer in Fiji, and who wrote an account of native beliefs regarding leprosy.[37] Although there are many obscure points in his article, reference must be made to it in this connection, since it appears that he obtained much of his information in the districts of Western Viti Levu. He writes, ". . . Fijian mythology is associated . . . with leprosy. There were in many districts, gods who were reputed lepers, and in others, gods who, though not lepers themselves, were held to preside in some way over leprosy. . . . Leprosy stones appear to be the shrines of *manes*, the outward visible sign by which occasionally the shades of leprous ancestors manifest their supposed power of communicating the disease to living persons. . . . They are treasured in particular families, generally leprous ones, the principal elder of which is by birth right, the officiating priest or wizzard who conjures the spirit."[38] After giving an account of three such stones near Rewa in Eastern Viti Levu, he mentions another in Noikoro, a district only a few miles to the East of Namataku. This stone is called *na vatu ni sakuka*, the "stone of leprosy" and is "a largish basaltic rock with peculiar markings upon it, in which the natives see a resemblance to the appearance of leprous maculae on the human skin. . . . The proprietor of this stone is considered to possess the attribute of conferring leprosy upon any offending person, whether of his own or of another *matagali*, and either of his own motion or in compliance with a petition and propiation offered by a third person. . . . Some person having by obnoxious actions or words given umbrage, the person offended would go to

---

[37] CORNEY (2).

[38] *Op. cit.* p. 11–12.

the *Taukei* (owner) of the leprosy stone and would entreat him to impart the disease to the proposed victim. At the same time he would make presentations of *yaqona*, whales teeth, *masi* or other property and these the functionary would offer up by placing them upon the stone and performing invocations (*vatonaka*) for a successful issue. He would then return to his dwelling and on *yaqona* being next prepared, he would, after drinking his portion . . . exclaim as his toast . . . 'Pfya! may his figure become as mine!' namely leprous; and speculation would of course, run high on this curse being uttered as to who might be the intended victim of the charm."[39]

Concerning a stone, or rather in this case a small cairn of separate stones, red in color, at Wala in the district of Namataku we have some additional information in the form of an account given by a boy who had been afflicted by leprosy: "Several years ago we went out . . . leaving the house empty . . . when we returned to the house we saw the Sakuka (leprosy) had crossed our threshold. He had put his mark there, he had entered at the end door and had crawled to the hearth; and we knew that he had been to our house because we saw his hand prints and foot prints in the ashes of the hearth . . . the feet were clubbed or hoof-like, and had lost their toes, and all were like the extremities of a leprous person . . . we knew that we should develop leprosy as a consequence . . . when I say the Sakuka marked our hearth I mean the demon of the stone. . ."[40]

Although over forty years have passed since these observations were made, it is strange that no notice of such stones was brought to my attention, except for the fact that they seem to be associated only with leprosy:[41] This disease was one which was very early attacked by the governmental medical authorities, and this fact might account for the present lack of magical practices connected with the production of it.

In concluding this discussion of native theories of disease causation, it may be pointed out that, as the material has revealed, the concept of *cause* is not a simple one. As Rivers remarked in

---

[39] Op. cit. p. 17-18.

[40] Op. cit. p. 21-23.

[41] Corney refers to a couple of "dropsy stones" but they appear to be found only in eastern Viti Levu. Op. cit. p. 24.

a passage which has already been quoted: "There are usually clear cut ideas concerning the immediate conditions which lead to the appearance of disease." These "immediate conditions" cannot, however, be said to be the cause, in the Fijian sense, of the disease. Let us take for example, the question of disease resulting from seduction, or attempted seduction by one of the *lewa nitu* who is acting at the instigation of the *vu* of the individual's clan. If in endeavoring to arrive at the native etiology of disease in this case one were to ask, "What was the cause of the illness?" cause would have to be translated by the Fijian word *vu* in its sense of source or origin, and by way of answer one would elicit (provided all the facts were known) not details of the seduction but an account of that action on the part of the individual that aroused the anger of the ancestral-spirit of his clan. It is similarly the case with diseases brought about by a sorcerer. Time after time, when collecting genealogies, I asked for the explanation of what seemed an untimely death, I was given details beginning with an account of the ultimate behavior of the individual which either provoked an angry attitude on the part of one of the *vu* or led to his extinction at the hands of a sorceror.

Although there is a danger of being too systematic in regard to native beliefs of this sort, is it not possible that the doubt and confusion existing in the minds of informants as to the inclusion of diseases resulting from sorcery and these due to failure to serve the *luveniwai*, within the category of *mate ni vanua*, may be due to the fact that all disease, with the exception of the *mate vayaŋo* is attributable ultimately, to unwise behavior on the part of individuals?

IV. Therapeutic Practices

Broadly speaking Fijian therapeutic practices may be divided into two main groups: (1) treatment administered for the immediate relief of the patient, the nature of which depends upon the symptoms; (2) measures adopted, where necessary, to deal with the ultimate cause of the disease. In case of illness thought or known to be the result of incidental circumstances, and involving no spiritual or human agency, practices of the first group are sufficient; while *mate ni vanua*, as well as diseases resulting from sorcery require additional measures, though in the cure of ailments belonging to these categories, recourse is also had to methods of healing of the first type.

Herbal Remedies

Foremost among remedies of the first group are the medicines of life. Like the medicines of death they are vegetable substances, usually leaves, though the root and the bark of the tree is sometimes used. I made a collection of specimens, representing only a sample of the plants known, and a list of native and botanical names with notes on the use of the plants will be found in the appendix. Although theoretically anyone may acquire a knowledge of herbal remedies and their proper application, actually very few natives avail themselves of their opportunitites to do so. In the village of Nasauthoko most of the inhabitants knew only one or two at most, and only one man, the Mbuli of Namataku, had a knowledge above the average. He had always been interested in the subject, he told me; his father had taught him many of the medicines and he had picked up information on the use of plants for medicinal purposes here and there as the opportunity offered. As a result he was frequently in demand, and his reputation based on numerous successes extended to other villages. I am indebted to him for many of the specimens in my collection. The *vuniwai* also has at his command a knowledge of a number of these medicines, and his knowledge, unlike that of the layman, is constantly being augmented by revelation, and his prescriptions in specific instances depend upon revelation; this will be discussed later when the *vuniwai* and his methods of treatment are considered.

According to one informant each of these medicines of life has a *tambu*: some article of diet is forbidden to the patient while he is being treated with the medicine. Another very good authority, however, stated that the *tambu* is imposed by the *vuniwai*, only in certain cases. After the patient has recovered he makes a bowl of *yaŋgona*, called *ne i sere* (the thing to break, or loosen), to the *vuniwai*, who then removes the *tambu*.[1]

Surgical Practices

Of decidedly secondary importance to herbal remedies are surgical practices. At the present time at least the only method of this nature is tatooing,[2] a practice adopted to cure muscular aches and pains. The instrument with which this is done is a short reed, about eight or ten inches in length, to one end of which are fastened four thorns. The pigment consists of soot scraped from the bottom of a cooking pot and mixed with a little water or coconut oil. The same pattern is always used; two or three horizontal stripes about a fourth of an inch wide and some two inches long one above the other are tatooed on the flesh in the region of the pain. The pigment is applied to the skin and the pattern impressed by tapping on the reed instrument to drive the thorns into the flesh. There is no ritual connected with this practise, if the patient is able to reach the spot he performs the operation himself, otherwise anyone may do it for him, as no special skill is required. Many of the women, especially the older ones, as might be expected from the nature of the ailments remedied in this way, have such marks, but both sexes resort to this mode of therapy. Informants were unable to give any reason underlying the procedure.

Judging from accounts of earlier writers surgical practices of another nature were formerly widespread throughout Western Viti

---

[1] In the Lau Islands the association of a *tambu* with each medicine is much more clearly defined (cf. HOCART (4), p. 163 et seq.), and it is possible that my information on this point is incomplete. P. E. ROUGIER, p. 1005, says that every remedy carries with it a tabu.

[2] Formerly women were tatooed extensively on the thighs and abdomen, and frequently around the mouth; but the art has declined and today, outside of its use in therapy, it survives only in the custom, practiced occasionally by women, of tatooing names of sweethearts or departed relatives on the chest or upper arm.

Levu, and it is probable that they were found in the region of Namataku, although to the best of my knowledge they do not occur at the present time. Dr. B. S. Corney[3] has discussed certain practices the primary object of which was blood-letting.[4] One of these, known as *thoka losi* "consists in passing a bougie or sound into the male urethra as far as the membraneous portion, and in making an incision about an inch in length upon it from without at the bulbous portion. A seton may or may not then be passed in at the wound, and out at the meatus, according to the whim of the operator.

"*Thoka losi* is done for various ailments or illnesses, generally in cases of lumbar rheumatism and in the sequelae of catarrhal fever, such as haric pneumonia, mild but painful pleuritis, and various neuralgic affections, and in disease of the sacro-iliac synchondroses.

"The usual explanation given by natives when interrogated as to the rationale upon which this operation is recommended is that by incising a dependent portion of the trunk, such as the perinaeum the abdomen is relieved from an accumulation of blood about its fundus. . . .

"The staff used is made generally from a twig of the tree called . . . losilosi. Hence the term employed for the whole operation, *thoka losi*, which means piercing with *losi*, . . . occasionally . . . a reed is made use of instead, and answers equally well, save that its point is less smooth and requires greater care in passing. The cutting instrument is generally a piece of sharp mussel or cockle shell . . . but occasionally a slip of bamboo. . . . The bast from the well-known vau tree, *Hibiscus tiliaceus*, forms a convenient seton, being tough and unirritating. . . ."[5]

Another remedial measure, also performed with a view to bloodletting, is known as *taya ŋgaleŋgale*.[6] This ". . . consists in incising the urethra at its meatus to a point just behind the froenum pre-

---

[3] CORNEY (1).

[4] Blood-letting though not as a cure for disease, strictly speaking, is resorted to frequently at the present day; when a child is about two or three years of age small horizontal cuts are made on its back, to let out the "bad blood" which it received from its mother before birth; whether or not the mother was healthy during pregnancy, her blood was probably bad from some mysterious cause. Bleeding is resorted to in case of sores which refuse to heal as well as internal disorders which do not respond to other treatment, according to ROUGIER.

[5] *Op. cit.*, p. 646 et seq.

[6] *Op. cit.*, p. 648.

putii, including division of its artery. This is allowed to bleed to an extent varying from a mussel shellful to a coconut shellful . . . half an ounce to a pint."[7] And he adds that "A cutting instrument is used for it similar to that employed in *thoka losi*, and in both the operators are men."[8]

Fison wrote of a "horrible surgical operation" which was performed in Western Fiji, "for any kind of wasting sickness, and the natives can give no reason for it nor explanation of it except 'our fathers did it'."[9] It appears from his accounts that it was very similar to the *taya ŋgaleŋgale* as described by Corney. Fison also mentions a method of treating females, though he does not say what were the diseases remedied in this way. "The female patient is laid down wide astraddle, in water, those regions [the genitals] being immersed. When the soaking is supposed to have continued long enough, she is laid on her back, the parts distended as far as possible, and then severely scraped with a slip of bamboo, the true Fijian *sele*, the word now used for knife . . . when the edge grew dull the operator tore off a small piece with his teeth leaving a new edge."[10]

Functions of the Vuniwai

Therapeutic practices of this first type are, as has been noted above, resorted to in treating disorders of all classes, whether *mate vayaŋo*, *mate ni vanua* or diseases resulting from sorcery. But in order that a patient suffering from ailments of the last two categories of causation may recover, additional measures must be taken. Since it is the part of the *vuniwai* first to discover to what category the particular disease belongs, and secondly to recommend the proper treatment, it is necessary to consider the nature and functions of his profession before discussing the therapeutic methods of the second type.

At the present time there are very few representatives of the profession in the northern districts of Tholo West.[11] Whether this is a recent condition due to attempts made by the government to

---

[7] *Op. cit.*, p. 648.
[8] *Ibid.*
[9] FISON (2), p. 439.
[10] *Ibid.*, p. 440.
[11] They are all men.

abolish such practices, by punishing the native doctors with jail terms and by supplying the districts with natives trained in European methods of therapy, cannot now be decided. At any rate, only one *vuniwai*, Setariki, a resident of the village of Sivikoso, was known to me personally. Although two or three others living at a distance were known in Nasauthoko by reputation and occasionally consulted, I had no opportunities to talk with them, and therefore depend for the following account upon the information supplied by Setariki. As will be seen later, the nature of the means by which the *vuniwai* acquires his skill permits individual variation in details, but it is probable that the fundamentals are similar in every case.

When I knew him, Setariki was a man about fifty years of age. Even upon first acquaintance it was obvious that certain definite and peculiar personality traits distinguished him from the average native. Among a group where personal appearance is a matter of daily concern, and a state of cleanliness considered essential, Setariki was habitually unkempt and very often quite noticeably unclean. My impressions were of a man of somewhat less than average intelligence even on occasions when it was not obvious that his wits were dulled with *yangona*.[12] The Fijians themselves, while with few exceptions[13] they relied implicitly upon his judgments, frequently spoke disparagingly of his general appearance and of his laziness and inefficiency as a gardener. But his devotion to his practice and his patients was complete, and, I am sure, entirely sincere.

Before giving the details regarding Setariki's career, some generalities concerning the profession of *vuniwai* may be stated. To begin with, the office of *vuniwai* is inseparable from that of *tolayandra* (*tola*, to see; *yandra*, vision), or seer;[14] or more correctly speaking in one of his functions the *vuniwai* is *tolayandra*, as the ability to see visions is perhaps the essential element in the practice of therapy according to the methods of the *vuniwai*. The abilities adhering to this office are derived from the association of the

---

[12] His profession entails the consumption of a considerable amount of *yangona*.

[13] Old Marika, of the Matatini clan and therefore one of the *i taukei* of the village, after Setariki had diagnosed Ruveni's death as due to failure of the subdivision of the clan to build a *mbito*, publicly and angrily denounced him as an ignorant imposter.

[14] Elsewhere in Fiji, judging from accounts of other writers, e.g. THOMSON, the priest-seer, called *mbete*, seems to be distinct from the *vuniwai*.

individual with one or more spirits, and therefore the *vuniwai* is distinguished from the layman who knows the medicines of life and how to administer them, by the fact that he has special spiritual powers, while the knowledge of the layman is mundane; and he is consequently far better fitted to deal with diseases contracted as a result of incurring the anger of the *vu*, or caused by sorcery.

All *vuniwai* have as their spiritual partners, *nitu* of the same name, *nitu ni vuniwai*, but other classes of spirits confer the powers pertaining to the function of *tolayandra*. There is some difference of opinion as to what classes of spirits these are. Setariki claimed to have acquired his ability to see visions from a spirit belonging to the group known as *mbete*, but Kitcioni was of the opinion that there are no *nitu* by this name, and that the word was a synonym for the *tolayandra* who actually obtained his powers from a *luveniwai* spirit. Others were equally positive in asserting that the *luveniwai* has nothing to do with this matter; but it may be noted that Sakenasa, an old man who in his youth had been a very active member of the *luveniwai* cult, informed me that on occasion a powerful *luveniwai* was able to take the place of the *vuniwai*. It seems apparent that circumstances vary in individual cases to such an extent that generalization is extremely difficult, or impossible; but it is also not unlikely that in these degenerate days, ignorance is responsible for the confusion.

Like all individuals who enjoy personal relationships with the *nitu*, the spirit is acquired involuntarily or through the instrumentation of another who himself possesses a spirit. The *vuniwai* in common with all others who "serve" spirits, is required to offer periodic oblations to his *nitu*, failure to do so resulting in disease. Setariki's daughter became ill because he neglected on one occasion to prepare *yaŋgona* for his spirits.

An account of the chief events leading up to the establishment of Setariki as a professional *vuniwai* illustrates these points. His first knowledge of the use of medicines of life was acquired from his father, Mbuketelau, who was himself a *vuniwai*.[15] For some time

---

[15] Although it is not unusual for fathers to instruct their sons, the office of *vuniwai* is not in any sense hereditary, at the present time at least. In this connection, however, it may be pointed out that BASIL THOMSON in replying to B. S. CORNEY's paper on Leprosy Stones in Fiji, said that "Therapeutic powers were hereditary; the secret of particular medicines was handed down from father to son, or mother to daughter . . ." (see *Folklore*, vol. 7, 1896, p. 25).

he treated disease as a layman but with very little success. One night, however, he felt a cramp in his foot, and recognized by this sign that *nitu* were present, and had come to abide with him. Altogether there were three, two *mbete* spirits named Tani ni vatu and Tani ni koro, as well as a *nitu ni vuniwai* named Soŋo na mate. All of these spirits had formerly been "served" by Saiyasi of Sivi-koso, who in addition to his activities as *ndau ndrondrotci*, had practiced the art of medicine. Saiyasi had died previously without having made the ceremony to send his spirits away, and they had come to Setariki, who made *yaŋgona* of welcome (*yaŋgona ni mata-karawa*) to them. The *mbete* spirits he said, conferred upon him the power of obtaining insight by means of the vision, and the *nitu ni vuniwai* instructed him in the knowledge and use of herbal reme-dies.[16] From this time on he was more successful in curing diseases and his fame began to spread abroad. Finally, after Setariki healed a girl in the province of Nandi who was suffering from a disease caused by the type of sorcery known as *mondroka*, Tomasi, a *vuniwai* from Noikoro, gave him another spirit, Erau, to guard the medi-cines. Since that time he has acquired a considerable reputation, and today his services are in great demand.

One of his most important functions is, by the process of diagno-sis, to determine the cause of the disease. Rivers has made the remark that "Although the nature of the belief in causation di-rectly determines the mode of treatment, the discovery of the cause usually needs no special rite. It is inferred immediately by the patient or his friends from their knowledge of acts, on the part of the patient which would have offended a man or spirit believed to have the power of inflicting disease."[17] This generalization how-ever does not hold for Fijian therapeutics. In spite of the fact that the nature of the causal factors does largely determine the method of therapy adopted, it is necessary first to know what these factors are, and the layman has no means at his disposal by which to discover them. We have seen that the external symptoms of the disease are no indication of the category to which it belongs, or in other words, the nature of the disease is not apparent from the

---

[16] This informant stated that all the medicines of life which are known today have been taught to mortals by the *nitu ni vuniwai*.

[17] RIVERS (3), p. 29.

symptoms. Nor is it possible correctly to infer the cause from a knowledge of acts of the patient which might have proved offensive to spirit or mortal, one reason for this being that disease is believed to be visited in many cases not upon the offender himself, but, it may be long after his death, upon one of his descendants, an innocent victim, who could not be expected to know the cause of his ailment. And it seems to me that a contributing element to the uncertainty of the patient is the fact that one large category of diseases, the *mate ni vanua*, are caused by the anger of the *vu* who are by no means consistent in meting out disease as a punishment for wrong-doing. Furthermore, the cause of the ailment might seem to be obvious, as when an individual cuts himself, and infection sets in, it is clear that his clumsiness with a knife resulted in the wound, but what here appears to be a result of incidental circumstances may be not accident, but design on the part of the *vu*. It is true that the layman is willing to hazard a guess as to the cause of any particular ailment, but he would not entertain the idea of acting upon it without professional advice, since he is very often proved to be wrong. When Ruveni died suddenly after a short illness there was considerable speculation regarding the cause of his disease. Several of his friends were inclined to regard it as a *mate vayaŋo*, due to change in climate, since he contracted the illness in Nausori, a village higher and noticeably cooler and more windy than Nasauthoko. Some others muttered vaguely of sorcery, recalling the fact that Ruveni had had difficulties with some men of another district over a certain financial matter. It remained for Setariki to diagnose the "real" cause, and to determine that the disease was a *mate ni vanua* caused by the *vu*. Various reasons were given to account for the condition of Losana, married two years and still childless, and therefore apparently barren: one man attributed it to the fact that Tevita, Losana's husband, was a disobedient son to his parents, continually disregarding their wishes; another theory was advanced by a woman, to the effect that Tevita and Losana probably cohabited every night, and as a result of such frequency "the blood came every month." But when he was requested to diagnose the case, the *vuniwai* was able to determine that the trouble was due to the "sins" of Tevita's old ancestors.

The processes of diagnosis are resorted to for a double purpose: first, to determine the nature of a particular disease; secondly, to reveal the cause of the ailment provided it is not found to be a *mate vayaŋo*. In order to discover whether or not a certain disease is a *mate vayaŋo*, the *vuniwai* lays his hands upon the patient, and if when he does this a cramp is felt in the big toe of his right foot, he knows that the disease is either a *mate ni vanua* or a result of sorcery; by another sign, if the pain passes from the patient's body into his hand, he knows that he is not dealing merely with a *mate vayaŋo*. According to an extension of this latter method, he is able to make deductions concerning the precise nature of the disease, aside from the general category into which it falls. For example, the group of ailments known as *sulua* (see p. 21) are recognized as such by the *vuniwai*, if when he touches the patient the pain extends to his elbow. In case the disease belongs to the group called *ŋwata*, the pain reaches to his shoulder, etc. It must be noted here that the method of diagnosis by touch is not a means of transferring the pain from the body of the patient to that of the *vuniwai*; to rid himself of the pain thus acquired the *vuniwai* places his hand on one of the house posts, into which the pain goes, but the patient is not relieved correspondingly.[18]

When it has once been determined that the disease is not a *mate vayaŋo*, it is necessary to discover the cause, so that the necessary measures may be taken to remove it. Otherwise, while disease caused by the anger of the *vu*, or by sorcery may be temporarily cured, it will recur. An individual, wishing to ascertain the cause of an ailment which he has contracted, or with which a relative is afflicted, takes a gift of *yaŋgona* to the *vuniwai* and asks him to diagnose the cause of the illness; in doing so he is said to "ask" the *vuniwai* "for life", to *taro mbula* (*taro*, ask; *mbula*, life).

There are at least two methods by which the *vuniwai* in the capacity of *tolayandra*, or seer, may reveal the cause of the disease.

---

[18] HOCART quotes an informant regarding a number of diseases of the abdomen: "They are all in the belly, but the names differ; it all depends on what is good for them (*kena yanga*); if a man is ill in the belly, they send for all those who know the names of diseases; they try one, then another; they come and touch (*vamotha*) the patient. If they touch the patient and he gets relief, they bring some medicine. It is our hand that is effective." Diagnosis by touch thus has a very different function here. HOCART sums the matter up by saying: "Thus diseases are not diagnosed by symptoms, but by the cure that happens to succeed. The mere touching can sometimes effect a cure apart from any remedies. Thus a boy of twelve was able to cure by touch internal pains in the ear and external swelling of the eye (*fuafua*). The power was hereditary, and came from his mother's father." The Lau Islands, pp. 161–162.

One procedure consists in gazing into a bowl of *yaŋgona*, in the shadows on the surface of which he is able to discern pictures of past events, and thus he discovers the conditions leading up to the illness, and the cause of the disease. Before gazing into the *yaŋgona* he makes a prayer to his spirits asking them to give him the power to interpret the shadows. A certain man whose grandson was ill consulted Setariki. In the *yaŋgona* the *vuniwai* saw the man holding up a whale's tooth, and this picture he interpreted as indicating that the man had kept for himself a *tambua* which should have been given to his clan. If as frequently happens, the patient himself does not consult the *vuniwai*, so that there is no opportunity to ascertain the nature of the disease by the method of touch, this may also be discovered by gazing into the bowl of *yaŋgona*; if the *vuniwai* sees nothing in the shadows he is able to state that the disease is a *mate vayaŋo*. Other instances of this method of diagnosis will be given later. Gazing into the *yaŋgona* is a means not only of revealing the cause of the disease, but its specific cure; very often the *vuniwai* sees in the shadows leaves of the proper medicine of life to be administered to the patient.

The process known as *vatakarakara*, translated by my interpreter as "imaginary thinking", in which the subject perceives in his mind a scene depicting events, is another means by which the *vuniwai* determines the cause of disease. This appears to be somewhat involuntary on the part of the subject; a cramp in the toe of his right foot indicates to the *vuniwai* that the picture is a true mirror of events, if in the toe of his left foot he knows that it is false.

Diagnosis to determine the cause of the disease may be practiced even after the death of the patient, a custom interrelated with the belief that the disease, provided the ultimate cause is not removed, may "jump" to a relative of the deceased. According to one method, when the body has been placed in the grave, and covered with earth, a stick is planted in the ground so that one end reaches down to the corpse, to be the path of the spirit. In the evening after the burial, a group of men repair to the grave, and one of them seizes the stick, saying, "A . . . (addressing the *yalo mate* of the dead person by name), take hold of the end of this stick while I pull." Then as he pulls up the stick the spirit of the dead man leaves the corpse and "enters" him. At this point, evidenced by the fact that the one thus "entered" begins to tremble and shake, his companions rush up and lay hold of him, asking the spirit to reveal the cause of the death. When they have received an answer, the spirit is told to return to the grave. This method of diagnosis was adopted when Nanewa, a man of Mbukuya, died, as a result of an illness for which no cause was known. His spirit when brought up from the grave, revealed that Nanewa had died as a result of sorcery made against him by Ratukini. Nanewa had thrown a stone accidentally hitting Ratukini in the head, as he was standing in the latrine, and Ratukini, incensed at this insult to his person, made *ne i ndrotci* and killed Nanewa.[19]

There is another method of attracting the *yalo mate* of a man who has died of an unknown cause, so that his spirit may be asked to impart information concerning the cause of death. A length of bamboo is placed so that one end of it is lying in the house where the man died, and the other end outside in the village. Several men stand beside the end of the bamboo which is outdoors, and direct the spirit which is thought to be in the house, to take hold of the bamboo, which is then pulled out of the house, and the spirit, clinging to it, comes out and "enters" one of the men. The *yalo mate* is asked to speak through the mouth of the man he has "entered", and to reveal the cause of death.[20]

It frequently happens that the spirit of its own accord visits one of the living shortly after the death of its owner. If an individual is heard moaning, other persons present recognize this as a sign that a spirit is visiting him, and a cord is tied around one of the house posts to detain the spirit until he has been questioned. Not only spirits of deceased persons visit mortals to give information concerning the cause of death, but very often the *nitu* who has been responsible for the death, by visiting one of the living and speaking through his mouth, makes known the reason for the act. Lewatu Momo herself revealed the circumstances of Eneri's death,[21] when she visited and spoke through the mouth of a clanswoman of his.

---

[19] Some insight is afforded into native attitudes towards the sorcerer by the fact that, when this became known, the villagers remonstrated with Ratukini, telling him that he should have contented himself with beating Nanewa.

[20] The belief that the spirit remains inside the house is not consistent with the idea found in connection with the method of diagnosis practiced at the grave of the dead man, but contradictions regarding such a point are probably to be expected.

[21] See p. 46.

Contrary to the emphasis placed on diagnosis, the art of prognosis is not developed in Fiji. As far as I know only the *luveniwai* deliberately sought knowledge concerning the outcome of illness.[22] A member of the society was able to prognosticate by means of his club[23] and fan;[24] these he placed upright without support on his arm, and sat with them in this position all night; if one of them fell off it was a sign that the patient would die, but if they remained upright until morning, he knew that the sick person would recover.[25]

It is said that to see the *yalo* of a living person is a forewarning of his death. Sight in such a case is different from ordinary vision: the "eyes are changed" in some way, not easily explained by the native, so that ordinary objects become invisible, while *yalo* and *nitu* which appear like mist may be discerned.[26] Theoretically anyone may have this experience, but it is more common for the *tolayandra* to see in this way. One informant was of the opinion that during illness the *yalo* frequently roams away from the body; another explained this by saying that a sick person sleeps more than ordinarily.[27]

Ceremonies of Propitiation

With this material on the nature and functions of the profession of *vuniwai* as introduction, we turn to the second group of therapeutic practices, comprising measures taken to deal with the ultimate cause of the disease. Since for ailments arising from incidental circumstances, therapeutic treatment of the first type is sufficient, we shall be concerned here only with *mate ni vanua* and diseases resulting from sorcery. For disease of either of these two types, with one exception, namely ailments caused by the anger of

---

[22] But WILLIAMS p. 146 writes, "The people near to Vatukali decide the question of a sick person's recovery by a visit to a famous *mulamula* tree, which is the index of death. If they find a branch of the tree newly broken off, they suppose that the person on whose account they pay the visit must die. If no branch is broken, recovery is expected."

[23] This club, or stick, is called *mothemothe*, the "bed" of the spirit, in which the *luveniwai* spirit resided.

[24] A reference to the fan used in the ceremony of initiation into the *luveniwai* cult; the individual being initiated is fanned and thus the spirit is wafted towards him.

[25] The ability to perform miracles of various sorts is possessed by all members of the cult.

[26] According to the Fijian expression they "strike the eye", *mata lau* (*mata*, eye; *lau*, to strike).

[27] The general theory is that the *yalo* departs during sleep.

human beings, spiritual assistance must be sought, though, as has been observed, remedies of the first class are not ignored.

The only method of obtaining such assistance is by means of the *i mandrali*, which is made on the prescription and under the direction of the *vuniwai*, who perceives the proper procedure for the ceremony usually at the same time as the cause of the disease is revealed to him. Though there is considerable variation in detail, some general features of the ceremony may be observed in every case. The *i mandrali* is usually composed of two items: the first, and indispensable one of these, is *yaŋgona*, a certain amount of which is poured out on the ground to the spirit whose aid is being sought; after this three or four men of those present, always including the one who presents and the one who accepts the *i mandrali*, and one or two others, are served with *yaŋgona*, and the remainder is shared among the men of the village who take it home to drink at their leisure. When the *i mandrali* is a small one *yaŋgona* only is offered, but at large ceremonies, it is accompanied by a presentation of food (*maŋiti*) consisting usually of pig, yams and taro. The pig and the *yaŋgona* are supplied by the individual who is making the ceremony, and women in the village provide the vegetables. None of the food is set aside for the *vu*, but after the ceremony it is distributed among the inhabitants of the village.[28] The *i mandrali* is formally offered with a speech of presentation explaining the circumstances of the offering, and is received with a speech of acceptance, by the *vuniwai* if he is present, or if not by someone who acts in his place.

All such ceremonies are substantially the same, but to cure an ailment belonging to the category of *mate ni vanua*, the *i mandrali* is made with a view to appeasing the wrath of the *vu* who has caused the disease, and is therefore offered primarily to him, though other spirits may be appealed to as well; while, if the disease has been brought about by witchcraft, the ceremony is not offered to the *vu* who owns the medicine, but is carried out by way of appealing to another spirit who is considered to have the power of controlling the influence of the medicine.

Accounts of several such ceremonies which I had opportunity to witness will illustrate these points.

---

[28] This general distribution is a feature of all feasts.

The *i mandrali* made by Tcolami who suffered from a badly infected foot, a *mate ni vanua* resulting from the anger of the *vu* because his ancestors had shed much blood in the old wars, is an example of an offering made to the *vu* who caused the disease. Tcolami's trouble began when, apparently by accident, he stumbled over a sharp stick lying on the path and cut his foot. As a minor wound of this sort is an everyday occurrence, he gave little thought to the matter until the wound failed to heal. He began then to apply herbal remedies and when I returned to the village after a short absence, he asked if my medicines would be of any help to him.[29] By this time the wound had closed while the infection was spreading to his leg, and I could offer no assistance. Later on the government doctor was summoned, but in spite of his medical skill the infection continued to grow worse. Finally when Setariki happened to be in the village, Tcolami consulted him and learned that he was suffering from a *mate ni vanua*, and that in order to recover he must make the *i mandrali* to the *vu* of his clan.[30] Setariki upon gazing into the bowl of *yaŋgona* had beheld two of Tcolami's ancestors holding spears in their hands. He therefore directed Tcolami to make an *i mandrali* consisting of six bowls of *yaŋgona*, this particular number being specified because six generations had intervened between Tcolami and the ancestors whose sin was responsible for the anger of the *vu*. These six bowls were divided into two divisions of three bowls each; one was termed *ne i mandrali ni ndra*,[31] the offering for the blood which had been shed; the second, *ne i mandrali ni wau*,[32] the offering for the weapons used. Each group consisted of three bowls, *ne i ŋgeti*,[33] the controller; *ne i mandrali*, the offering; *ne i tharatharamaki*,[34] that which

---

[29] I frequently applied iodine, when permitted by the natives, to minor cuts and wounds.

[30] It is probable that he consulted the *vuniwai* only as a last resort because of the fact that he was an ardent Christian. However he was not one to withhold from the "devil" his due, and he took pains to point out to me when after making the ceremony he rapidly recovered, that the *vuniwai* had succeeded where the government doctor had failed.

[31] *ndra*, blood.

[32] *wau*, a kind of war club.

[33] The verb is *ŋgetia*, an old word no longer used in ordinary speech. It is said literally to mean "to pull back" in the sense of removing; here it refers to the "old deeds of the ancestors, so that they will not occur again in the future."

[34] From *tharamakinia*, used of clearing away rubbish of any sort, also of clearing the ground for a garden, of weeding, etc.

clears away. The *maŋiti* in this case was composed of a pig and yams. After the ceremony had been presented by Tcolami and accepted by Setariki on behalf of the *vu* of the clan, two bowls, *ne i tharatharamaki* of each division, were poured out to the *vu*.

Failure to pour the libation in making the ceremony was itself the cause of illness in the following case. When Ratumeli, a man from Nalembalemba, was ill while visiting in Nasauthoko, he was directed to offer the *i mandrali* to the *vu* of his clan whom he had angered by giving away a *tambua* without making an *i mandrali* for it. When this was made, Setariki, who was in charge of the case, told Semi to pour out one of the bowls to Erau, the spirit who guarded the medicines of the *vuniwai*. But this Semi neglected to do, and as a consequence, his wife, Lusiana, was afflicted with a severe headache and Natheva, his daughter, suffered a swollen thigh. Setariki was consulted and, gazing into the bowl of *yaŋgona* he saw Erau standing among four bowls of *yaŋgona*. Whereupon he directed Semi to make an *i mandrali* consisting of four bowls, *ne i ŋgeti, ne i mandrali, ne i tharatharamaki*, and *ne i sava*,[35] the washer; the fourth bowl was to be poured out to Erau.

The illness of Lotu, which was caused by witchcraft, aside from its interest as an example of disease for the cure of which an *i mandrali* was made, affords an illustration of more than one important point which came up for consideration in the discussion of disease resulting from sorcery, and will therefore be presented in some detail. The history of this illness extends far back in the past. Long ago in Mbukuya there lived a man named Raturusiati. One day he went away on a journey, leaving no one at home except his wife. During his absence, she was seduced by Ulunikatikati, whose home was also in Mbukuya. While they were lying together, Vutuwaŋgewaŋge, the brother of Raturusiati, came into the house and found them. As he entered by one door, Ulunikatikati escaped by the other, but when the woman tried to run away, Vutuwaŋgewaŋge speared her in the thigh. Early the next morning Raturusiati returned to Mbukuya, and as soon as he arrived in the village, his brother related the story of the affair to him. On that day Ulinikatikati, together with some clansmen, was working in his garden. just as they were sitting down to rest and eat at noon, Raturusiati

---

[35] From *savatcia*, to wash.

appeared. He rushed at Ulunikatikati; he caught hold of him, pulled his hair and finally knocked him flat on the ground. When Ulunikatikati's clansmen saw what was happening, they seized Raturusiati and began to beat him with a stick, but while they were thus occupied, Vutuwaŋgewaŋge arrived upon the scene, bringing with him his gun and some bullets. He took aim, but as he was about to fire, they saw him and fled, plunging into the river which bordered the gardens. Before Vutuwaŋgewaŋge could hit any of them, they were across the river and disappearing into the bush. From that day on they never returned to the village; they built shelters for themselves in the bush where they slept and ate their meals.

Beginning with that episode, Ulunikatikati and Raturusiati and all their relatives and descendants hated each other. One day not long after this Rambalambala, a brother of Ulunikatikati, went to Sautambu, a village on the Siŋatoka river, where his mother's brother lived. He took with him three whale's teeth, which he presented to his uncle, asking for some medicine with which to make magic against Vutuwaŋgewaŋge. There they taught him the method of *ne i ndrotci* called *mbelo*, and when he had learned the procedure he returned to Mbukuya. Having stolen Vutuwaŋgewaŋge's turban of barkcloth, he put it with the leaves and a little water into a clay pot. When he had made a fire he set the pot on it, and as the water began to boil, Vutuwaŋgewaŋge began to gasp for breath, and within a short time he was dead. About two years after this, the power of the *mbelo* jumped to Raturusiati and he also died. However Rambalambala neglected to make the *i mandrali* to the spirit who controls the *mbelo*, and he himself contracted a disease. But before he died he called to his side Tcathoro, the son of Ulunikatikati and passed on to him the knowledge of the *mbelo* magic. "Look here, my son," said he, "When I am dead, do you take my place in killing those people whom we hate, those of Raturusiati's clan." Three years later Tcathoro killed Vutuwaŋgewaŋge's son, Vetheli, by this method; and Tevita, the son of Raturusiati died also when the power of the medicine jumped to him. Vetheli's brother, Lorima, escaped the same fate because he had been given a medicine of life to control the *mbelo* by a man in the province of Mba. But another Lorima, the son of Tevita's brother, Newato, succumbed to the medicine, and died suddenly.

After burying Lorima, Newato started back to Mbukuya, but on his way he began to feel weak and feeble, and was forced to stop in Vaturu, where he too died, another victim of the *mbelo*. One week later the daughter of the first Lorima, the man who was protected against the *mbelo* by his medicine of life, died. A short time after this, Tcathoro himself died, like his father's brother before him, as a result of failure to make the *i mandrali* for the medicine of death. The power of the *mbelo* however continued, and Lotu, a boy of fifteen or sixteen years of age, a son of the first Lorima, began to be afflicted with recurrent attacks of disease, a swelling which appeared first in his hand, then in his back, and finally in his shoulder. At this point Setariki was called in and asked to diagnose the cause of the disease. After *yaŋgona* had been prepared, the *vuniwai* gazed into the bowl, in the shadows on the surface of which there appeared first a bamboo containing the *i ndrotci*; a bit later Tcathoro, Vetheli, and Tevita took shape; and finally all vanished together. The girl who was to serve the *yaŋgona* took a coconut shell cup, and, to stir up the sediment in the bottom of the bowl, dipped the liquid and poured it back before serving it. As the stream of *yaŋgona* fell back into the bowl, Setariki watched closely, and saw at first faintly, then more clearly, the leaf of the medicine of life to be administered to his patient. Later on that night the details of the *i mandrali* to be offered were revealed to him in a vision, and under his direction the ceremony took place the following day.

Three large bowls of *yaŋgona* and a basket of yams were placed in a row, and the basket was flanked on each side by a small bowl of *yaŋgona*. These were named as follows: The three large bowls were *ne i ŋgeti, ne i mandrali, ne i tharatharamaki*; the basket of yams was *ne i sava*; the two small flanking bowls were *ne i soŋo*, the controller,[36] and *ne i mbula ni rau ni kai* the burying of the leaf.[37]

Vaula, an old man from Sivikoso who had accompanied Setariki to Nasauthoko, offered the *i mandrali*, as Lotu as too young to know how to make the speech. His words of presentation are typical.

ne i mandrali so okwe ni rau ni kai me, kondaki miti kilatcia rewa,
the offering   this of leaf of tree   as   you know able

---

[36] This refers to controlling the medicine of death.
[37] That is, the medicine of death.

na kea i ŋgeti, na kea i mandrali, na kea i vavuto,[38] *na*
the of it remover the of it offering   the of it cleanser   the

kea maŋiti. tovoli koto na kea i roŋo.[39]
of it feast telling   the of it news

Setariki, in accepting, made the following speech:

ŋgi lai tambakia ŋa ne i mandrali. me kua ni yatho tale na
I go to touch   the offering to not   arrive again the

kea nduka, me soŋo ne i ndrotci, me kua ni yatho tale na
of it evil to control the medicine to not   come again the

kea nduka i vuaru e ya luve.   me tini valiaŋa, me thola o Lotu.
of it evil to them the children to end once   to live Lotu

mana, e . . . ndjina.[40]
mana   it is true

When the *i mandrali* had been accepted Setariki was served a
cup of *yaŋgona* from the bowl termed *ne i ŋgeti*, and then Vaula
was given a cup from the bowl called *ne i mandrali*; *ne i soŋo*, and
ne i mbula ni rau ni kai were poured out to Erau, one of the *vuniwai's*
spirits. The ceremony was concluded by sharing the yams among
the people of the village.

A similar *i mandrali* was made to cure Lemeki who also suffered
from a disease caused by sorcery. Some time previously as Mbuli
of the district of Namataku, he had, without consulting those to
whom it belonged, transferred a portion of land from one *yavusa*
to another,[41] and by this act so enraged the owners that they made
ne i ndrotci against him, which caused him to become insane. Once
before, the ceremony of *i mandrali* was made to restore him to

---

[38] Refers to the act of putting something in the water to be taken away by the current.

[39] "This is the *mandrali* for the leaf, as you well know, the remover of it, the offering for it, that which washes it away, and the feast for it. I am telling the news of it."

[40] "I am accepting the *mandrali*, in order that the evil will not return, in order to control the medicine, so that the evil will not return to the children. Let it be finished once and for all. May Lotu live. Mana! it is true." In both speeches there are archaic words and unusual phrasings, and exact translations, word by word, are therefore difficult to make. The last phrase, "*Mana e . . . ndjina!*" is uttered at the end of any speech of acceptance; *mana* here is untranslatable.

[41] Being a government official he was in a position to record the transfer in the books. It will be remembered that according to Fijian custom, land is inalienable.

sanity, but without satisfactory results, and several years afterwards Tevita, his son, decided to consult another *vuniwai*. He went this time across the river to the village of Ndraumbuta where he received directions to make another ceremony. The *yaŋgona* for this *i mandrali* was contained in a hundred receptacles, for the most part lengths of bamboo about a foot long, cut so that the internode formed a bottom for the container, and forked so that they could be stuck into the ground. These were divided into four groups, *ne i ŋgeti, ne i mandrali, ne i tharatharamaki*, and *ne i vatataili*,[42] (that which sends away). In addition to this a *maŋiti* consisting of a pig, yams and taro was provided. Since Tevita, who was making the ceremony, did not know how to present it, this was done by Anasa, of Nausori, who stood in the relationship of classificatory mother's father to Tevita. And as the *vuniwai* under whose direction the ceremony had been made, was not present, it was accepted by Ratusireli, chosen, according to a vague statement, because his ancestors in the old days had served in the capacity of *vuniwai*. One receptacle from each group was poured out to the spirits, but no one present was sure as to which spirits these were. It is probable that this ignorance was due to the absence of the *vuniwai* on this occasion.

In addition to prescribing the *i mandrali* as a means of propitiating specific spirits, when he is personally attending the patient the *vuniwai* makes a prayer every morning and evening during the course of the illness, to all the spirits. A bowl of *yaŋgona* is prepared, a cup of which is poured out as an offering, *ne i sevusevu*, and through this medium the *vuniwai* prays to the spirits, asking that the sick person be healed, and all other people be sheltered from every disease.

It has already been mentioned that the *i mandrali* must be made in all cases of *mate ni vanua* except those resulting from the anger of a living person. To cure an illness of this type it is necessary for the patient to perform an act of propitiation of another sort, to the person whose anger has caused the disease. This act or offering is called *ne i soro* (see p. 29). When a disease is diagnosed by the *vuniwai* as the result of the anger of another individual,

---

[42] The verb is *vatatailitcia*, to dismiss or send away. It has reference here to the spirit who owned the medicine of death used in making the *i ndrotci*.

he directs the type of *i soro* to be made. To cure the illness which was caused by the anger of Tcolami, her father-in-law, Nanewaŋga (see p. 28) was told by the *vuniwai* to offer an *i soro* to Tcolami, consisting of a pig and a bowl of *yaŋgona*. The *yaŋgona* in such a case has no name corresponding to those for the bowls presented in the ceremony of *i mandrali*, nor is the *yaŋgona* poured out to any spirit, this being an affair involving humans only.

The offering of *ne i soro* of another type, also with the idea of propitiation, and also in connection with the cure of disease, has been described by Fison in his discussion of the Nanga rites.[43] "When a man of note is dangerously ill, a family council is held and it is agreed that a circumcision shall take place as a propitiatory measure. Notice having been given to the priests, an uncircumcised lad—the sick man's son or one of his brother's sons—is taken by his kinsman to the *vale tambu* or god's house, and there presented as a *soro*, or offering of atonement, that his father may recover. His escort makes valuable presents of property at the same time, and promises of more. These are graciously received by the priest, who sets a day on which the operation is to be performed. In the interval no food may be taken from the plantations except what is absolutely required for everyday use, no pigs or fowls may be killed, and no coconuts plucked from the trees. . . .

"On the day appointed the son of the sick chief is circumcised, and with him a number of other lads whose friends have agreed to take advantage of the occasion. Their foreskins, stuck in the cleft of a split reed are taken to the Nanga, and presented to the chief priest, who, holding the reeds in his hand, offers them to the ancestral gods, and prays for the sick man's recovery."[44]

---

[43] Although as I have mentioned elsewhere it is possible that the *naŋa* cult as described did not extent into the region of Namataku, I have included FISON's account for the sake of illustrating the importance of propitiation in Fijian therapeutics.

[44] FISON (2), p. 27. This act of course conflicts with the statements of my informants that the *i soro* was never made to spirits. THOMSON (2) p. 157, was assured by his informants that "the rite was in no way connected with sacrifice for the sick" and certainly at the present day, as far as I am aware, circumcision is never resorted to for this purpose, but BREWSTER on the other hand states (1) p. 310, "According to the native chronicler, sickness was the cause of circumcision. It was a sacrificial act made to appease and avert the wrath of the ancestral gods. When a man got infirm and old, and sickness got such a hold on him that he could not shake it off, he would say, 'I have sinned against the Lawa Ruku; [in a footnote he says this term refers to the "canons and ordinances laid down by religion"]; therefore I must make a sacrifice' (called in Noikoro *moko nai soro*). Then he would get one of his younger

We are also told that "Every member of the Nanga has the privilege of approaching the ancestors at any time. When sickness visits himself or his kinsfolk, . . . he may enter the Nanga with prayer and reverence and deposit on the dividing wall his whale's tooth, or bundle of cloth . . . and having thus recommended himself to the dead he may invoke their powerful aid."[45]

For the cure of disease resulting from failure to fulfil obligations, in addition to recommending that an *i mandrali* be made, the *vuniwai* usually directs the patient to compensate for the negligence. Thus Kitcioni, when his illness was diagnosed as due to the fact that his father had not properly requited those who had given him his *rere* spirit (see p. 31) was directed by the *vuniwai* to call together all the old people in the village and to make a feast for them. And the man whose ancestors had neglected to recompense the people of Toŋe in return for shelter (see p. 27), made a feast by way of payment when he learned the cause of his illness.

Confession as a Therapeutic Practice

Before leaving the discussion of therapeutic practices, it is necessary to mention the beneficial effects derived from confession[46] of sin, sin in this case usually referring to transgressions of a sexual nature.[47] Although the disease is not thought to result from such acts, therapeutic treatment of whatever sort will not prove effective until the patient has confessed his sin, regardless

relatives and one of his sons to go through the rite of circumcision as an act of atonement." Brewster, although Fijians informed him that the foreskins were thrown away, thinks that they were lying and that actually they were presented as offerings.

[45] *Op. cit.*, p. 26.

[46] BREWSTER (2) p. 98, has also noted this fact. "Under the old law and at the present time, open confession is the best remedy for transgressors. Sin is the cause of so many ailments, which are aggravated by concealment. Therefore people on beds of sickness are always exhorted by their relatives and friends to make clean breasts of their short-comings. But those in such circumstances very often are unable to make a wholesome survey of their past and magnify the veriest peccadilloes into deadly sins. I have known a whole community set by the ears by the morbid confession of a dying woman who turned her harmless and innocent flirtations and friendships into something infinitely worse." It is significant, I think, that while referring to sin in general, BREWSTER has in mind, apparently, sexual sin in particular, and this is in accordance with conditions prevailing in Namataku. Another reference to confession in connection with disease is to be found in Rev. W. DEANE's book, p. 144.

[47] RAFFAELE PETTAZZONI in his study of confession has pointed out that confession generally takes place in connection with sickness (p. 130) and that, "Dans la grande majorité des cas on constate . . . que seuls sont objet de confession des péchés sexuels . . . " (p. 134).

of the category of the disease. To confess is to *thavutcia*, literally to mention, and the patient is required to name his partner or partners in sin. When Ruŋua, a girl from Ndraimba, was ill, Setariki, who was attending her, asked her if she had anything to "mention," and she named two young men who had cohabited with her. Not only the *vuniwai*, however, acts as confessor, but anyone may take it upon himself to prompt the patient to *thavutcia*. Sakiusa had aroused considerable ill-feeling against himself when he denied, after the girl had confirmed the general suspicion, that he had cohabited with Vulori; when he was suffering from influenza, one of the men in the village went in to visit him, and emerged from the house, rather triumphantly it must be admitted, after having elicited a confession from the patient.[48]

Ceremonies Performed upon Recovery

There remain to be discussed the ceremonies performed by the patient upon recovery. At least once during his illness, the women of the village have made him a ceremonial presentation of food termed *sasala*, in accepting which he made a bowl of *yaŋgona* to welcome them. When he has fully recovered he makes a feast, *ne i thele ni latc*[49] to all those who have been of assistance to him throughout this time. Such a feast should consist of a pig and vegetables, and of course, *yaŋgona*. Tcolami, when the infection in his foot had healed, made a feast, but provided only *yaŋgona* and a platter of nuts; there was some grumbling on this occasion over the lack of better provision.

Another feast, *ne i tharatharamaki*, is made when his work is finished to the *vuniwai*, or rather to his spirits to whom a libation of *yaŋgona* is poured out. According to his own statement the *vuniwai* does not always receive payment in addition to this. He was given nothing for attending Lotu in his illness, though he had spent two or three weeks in Nasauthoko with his patient; nor did Tcolami make him any payment. Semi, on the other hand, after he had cured Lusiana and Natheva, gave him a bottle of coconut oil, and on another occasion he was given a horse.

---

[48] In order to facilitate delivery in a prolonged and difficult labour, the woman is frequently asked if she has anything to confess.

[49] Literally the removal of the straw. This refers to replacing the dried grsss beneath the mats on which the sick person had lain, with a fresh supply.

V. Conclusion

When we examine these concepts of disease against the background provided by the introductory material, it will become apparent to what extent the beliefs in causation and the therapeutic practices are interrelated with various social and religious aspects of Fijian culture. It is not probable, I think, that this relation was the same formerly as today, after half a century of European influence brought to bear upon aboriginal conditions by both church and state. However, even today a considerable degree of integration exists between these several phases of native culture.

Especially in the beliefs regarding the type of act which results in disease, can the sociological factor be discerned. A survey of the material reveals the fact that in many cases illness resulted from failure to fulfil obligations to one's fellowmen, or from failure to conform to standards of behavior set up by society. Among such cases are those in which disease was contracted as a consequence of acts which aroused the anger of fellow human beings. Instances will be recollected in which sickness was the penalty for failing to make payment for services rendered, for example, the case of the man whose ancestors had been sheltered by the people of Toŋe. It is not by accident that in so many examples a girl was afflicted with disease as a punishment for refusing to marry a man whose clan-fellows had made the ceremony of betrothal to her *mataŋgali*. Not only is it considered an insult for a suitor to be rejected, but it is a real economic loss to his clansmen: they have supplied the necessary gifts to be presented to the members of the girl's clan, for which they receive no return; and these gifts are not refunded by her people if the girl refuses her consent to the match. In the old days such a situation frequently led to warfare, and it seems possible that restrictions on such satisfactory means of obtaining revenge, has led to added importance of more subtle methods, and that in the past cases of disease resulting from like circumstances were more rare.

Retribution for offenses against the socially established order is in some cases in the hands of the *vu* of the *mataŋgali*, who is interested in the welfare of his human descendants; and in other instances, in the hands of the offended individual himself, who to obtain revenge, may call upon the *vu* of his clan to aid him or he may have recourse to magical means.

It is possible that formerly other features of the social organization might have been of some importance in the problem of disease. We have seen, for example, that in this region today, the only objects associated with the clans are, with few exceptions, of a vegetable nature, and that where edible or otherwise serviceable, there is no restriction on their use by members of the *mataŋgali*. We have, however, certain hints that in neighboring localities, at least in the past, each *mataŋgali* was associated with an animal as with certain plants, and that this animal was forbidden as food to members of the clan. Breach of this tabu resulted in sickness. Rivers (1), whose remarks refer specifically to the people of Nandrau, in the province of Tholo North, writes, "In this and other tribes of the interior, a man respects the animal of his mother as well as that of his father. . . . I was told of an interesting instance of the evil effects believed to follow non-observance of these restrictions. A man whose people had always eaten snakes, married a woman to whom these animals were *tambu*. He did not give snakes to his children but their food was cooked in pots that had been used to cook snakes and the constant illness of his children was ascribed to this cause, and in order to escape from continual trouble he left his wife and took another woman."[1] A somewhat similar case in which the flesh of a certain animal was *tambu* as food to members of one *mataŋgali* was brought to my attention. Semi whose original home was in Naveauŋo, in the district of Ŋgalimare, south of Namataku reported that the *vu* of his clan frequently took the form of a shark and that the members of his clan were forbidden to eat shark or food cooked in a pot which had been used for cooking shark; and that the penalty for doing so was disease. In any case at the present time in Namataku, regardless of possible conditions in the past, disease is not attributed to offenses of this nature.

It is obvious that the fear of disease has been in the past, and is

---

[1] (2), Vol. i, p. 273.

still today, a positive component in the motivations that uphold custom and the social structure. If the interdependence of various aspects of the social system and the beliefs regarding disease have helped to preserve, in a changing world, the native theories and practices centering around disease situations, it has also been of importance in maintaining many elements of the aboriginal social order which might otherwise have died out.

It is in terms of the religious ideology of these people, however, that the concepts of disease have specific and distinctive meaning. In both the factors of causation and the therapeutic methods, may we discern the close relationship between these concepts and religious beliefs. The position of the *vu* with regard to causal factors may be summed up briefly. The large category of diseases, comprising those known as *mate ni vanua* are considered to be directly due to the anger of the *vu*. The ancestral spirit of the clan is responsible for inflicting disease in some cases, as a penalty for failure to perform certain duties or to fulfil obligations, both those involving other human beings, and those which are regarded as matters concerning the individual and the *vu* of his clan; in other instances the *vu* acts to revenge some insult or offense to one of the members of the clan. Other *vu* as well, in addition to those who are the spirit ancestors of the various *mataŋgali*, inflict disease upon human beings. Illness may result from negligence in the matter of serving the spirit on the part of those who have entered into personal relationships with any of the *vu*.

Even in the production of disease by sorcery where the agent is a human being, the *vu* who are regarded as owning the medicines of death, play an important role.

In therapeutic practices the most prominent position is that held by the *vuniwai*. His powers are obtained from spirits whom he serves, and are of a religious rather than a secular nature. As we have seen religious practices in this part of Fiji are based upon the theory that personal relationships are possible between individuals and spirits, and that from these relationships powers of a super-ordinary nature may be acquired by mortal men. The *vuniwai* therefore takes his place in Fijian society with all others who derive special abilities and skills from their associations with the *nitu*.

Highly significant as an indication of the intimate relationship between religion and thereapeutic practices is the fact that one of the most important items in the treatment of disease is the ceremony of *i mandrali* made in some cases to propitiate the *vu* who has caused the disease, and in others to appeal to the *vu* for aid. The *i mandrali* as we have seen is not made only in connection with the cure of disease, but is an important ceremonial procedure in other enterprises where it is necessary to obtain the favor of the *vu*.

Disease as a Sanction in Fijian Society

Disease, then, functions in Fijian society as a religious sanction. The frequency with which in primitive societies as a whole, disease performs this function suggests that it is by nature, peculiarly suited to this role. In any society disease is of sufficiently common occurrence to meet the requirements of a sanction which acts to uphold social mores and its interpretation in these terms offers an explanation of and a means of dealing with situations inherently fraught with anxiety. Furthermore, the fact that in the majority of cases disease is not fatal allows a continued faith in the methods of therapy adopted, thus adding directly to the force of the sanction.

However, any society which utilizes disease for this purpose is faced with certain problems, on the solution of which depends the value of the sanction. It is in solving these problems in terms of its own social and religious ideology that each society makes its unique contribution to the study of disease as a sanction.

Theoretically the number of customs and mores under a disease sanction should not be either too great or too small in proportion to the general incidence of disease, since in the one case many infractions of the rules would obviously not result in illness; and in the other, a large number of occurrences of disease could not be interpreted in terms of wrong-doing. Either of these conditions would lead to a weakening of the sanction. It might be supposed therefore, that, in societies where, due to climate and geographical location the general incidence of disease is high, there will be found a greater variety of customs under a disease sanction than in comparatively healthy regions. Such a correlation is actually of course far too automatic and fails to take into account the fact that a balance can be and is, in societies for which we have adequate information, maintained by cultural factors. Thus, it is

obvious that in a locale where the incidence of disease is high the
culture may discount for the purposes of the religious sanction a
number of ailments, which may then be explained in other terms:
an example is the use of sorcery in many societies to accomplish
this end. Even where it would seem that the number and variety
of types of acts under a disease sanction must be overwhelmingly
greater than the probable incidence of disease, the disproportion
may be rectified by the culture in a number of ways: in certain
Polynesian societies the sum total of taboos reinforced with fear
of disease would seem to have been too great to allow for the
proper functioning of the sanction, had not the culture provided
the necessary mechanisms to relieve the transgressor of the danger
resulting from infringement.

Let us examine Fijian concepts of disease and its causation in
the light of this theory of a necessary balance between causes and
effects. To begin with, of the large body of regulations and prohibitions established by society not by any means all are placed
under a disease sanction; violations of incest taboos and disregard
of the rules of exogamy are not, apparently[2], thought to be
punished by disease. The relatively limited number of mores under
a disease sanction is however capable of expansion due to certain
components in the complex of beliefs relating to disease. We have
seen that individuals may suffer for the sins of their fathers into
remote generations. Obviously such a belief enlarges very con-
siderably the extent to which disease may be attributed to wrong-
doing. It is also an important factor in the interpretation of diseases of infants and children who have themselves had very little
if any opportunity to provide the *vuniwai* with explanations in
terms of transgressions. There is also a certain vagueness inherent
in the concept of the *vu* as punitive agents. As I have pointed out,
there is nothing automatic in the relationship between the transgression and the punishment; but the determining factor is a
variable—namely, the anger of the *vu*. Since in the series of cases

---

[2] In the course of my field work over 50 cases of disease came up for discussion in various
connections. In none of these were infractions of incest taboos or of rules of exogamy concerned. Informants, asked whether such infractions ever resulted in disease, replied in the
affirmative but could cite no examples. When I put the question in another form and asked
what happened to those who married within the forbidden kinship categories, I was told
that such marriages were likely to be sterile.

which were brought to my attention certain infractions occur time and again, we may infer that the types of transgressions thought to arouse the anger of the *vu* are rather clearly defined. But, theoretically at least there is nothing to prevent the *vuniwai* from making original interpretations, thus adding to the traditional types. Furthermore we have seen that it is not always necessary for the *vuniwai* to be very specific in his diagnoses; nothing could be more general than the statement that Tcolami's infected foot was due to the fact that his ancestors had shed too much blood in the old wars. The belief that illness is due to the anger of living individuals also contributes to the degree of elasticity in the number of mores under a disease sanction. The *vuniwai* is able to attribute disease to almost any quarrel or dispute, however slight, in which the patient had been involved. All of these concepts operate, it seems to me, to increase sufficiently to meet the requirements of the sanction, the number of regulations and prohibitions reinforced with a fear of disease.

When we examine the methods by which the Fijians handle disease situations in general, we observe certain cultural factors at work to reduce the number of occurrences of disease to be interpreted in terms of the sanction. It will be remembered that one category of disease, the *mate vayaŋo* (diseases of the body) are regarded casually and considered to be the result of incidental circumstances. In addition, very little attention is paid to a large number of ailments—those of old people; and a condition such as blindness which would be a cause for serious concern in a youthful individual is taken more or less as a matter of course among the aged. Finally since there is no hard and fast line drawn between the *mate vayaŋo* and the *mate ni vanua* on the basis of the nature of the disease, the *vuniwai* is at liberty if he is not aware of any transgression to make a diagnosis of any given case in terms of casual conditions. Thus one of the most important factors in maintaining the balance between causes and effects in disease is the function of the *vuniwai* as final arbiter.

It seems to be almost universally true that in societies where disease functions as a sanction, it is usually assumed that sickness is remediable and that the methods of therapy which make use of such devices as propitiation or expiation, or in some way attempt to remove the cause of the trouble, are effective. If then, the sanction is to maintain the strength of its hold, the complex of beliefs must embody some explanation for the cases of incurable disease, and above all for the cold fact of death. Obviously failure in this respect will not allow a proper reliance in the therapeutic practices.[3]

What then are the means adopted in Fijian culture to resolve this difficulty? In the first place, a large percentage of those deaths which occur do not require, according to Fijian belief, an explanation or interpretation in terms of the disease sanction: when an individual reaches an advanced age his infirmities are regarded as inevitable, and when death occurs no attempt is made to consult a *vuniwai* regarding the cause. But aside from such cases all deaths, including those of very young children are considered as resulting from *mate ni vanua*.[4] When the individual is dead, therefore, there is no question regarding the nature of his illness. However as we have seen, it is impossible to assign any disease on the basis of its symptoms to a certain category. Consequently especially in the present day, a disease may optimistically be assumed to be a *mate vayaŋo*, in which case the *vuniwai* is not consulted. Actually of course even in such cases death may occur suddenly and it is only at this point that the *vuniwai* will be asked to investigate the matter. In a certain proportion of the deaths that occur, therefore, no strain is imposed on the belief in the efficacy of the therapeutic practices since no test of their power was involved.

It is inevitable however that a number of patients under the care of the *vuniwai* will succumb to disease even after all the prescribed measures have been carried out. What then are the explanations advanced by the Fijians to account for this fact? In order to give a thoroughly satisfactory answer to the question it would be necessary to have information regarding a number of such cases. However, the various reasons put forth for the failure of the therapeutic measures in the case of Lemeki (see p. 63) are illuminating and probably indicative of the general trend of Fijian theories on the subject. One informant was of the opinion that Lemeki did not recover his sanity after the *i mandrali* had been made because

---

[3] Unfortunately we know very little regarding this subject for most primitive societies. But excellent information is given by R. FORTUNE for the Manus of the Admiralty Islands, pp. 352–3.

[4] For the moment at least, I am including in this category, diseases attributed to sorcery.

the land had not been returned to its original owners.[5] Another man suggested that perhaps someone had been overlooked in the distribution of food which followed the ceremony. It was also stated that probably the *vuniwai* was at fault, that due to failure on his part to serve his spirits properly they had not instructed him correctly when consulted.[6] All of these reasons are intelligible and perfectly plausible when considered in the light of Fijian therapeutic theory and practice. The necessity for making restitution for wrongs committed has already been mentioned (see p. 64). The distribution of food provided for the *i mandrali* is an established custom (e.g., see p. 58). Finally the idea that the *vuniwai* must serve his spirits or suffer the consequences is thoroughly in accordance with the general beliefs regarding the relations between individuals and their spirit-helpers. Indeed, one of my best informants on these matters stated categorically that, in cases where the patient failed to recover, the *vuniwai* was at fault. To a certain extent of course, complete reliance on the special powers of the *vuniwai* is one aspect of the faith in therapeutic practices; but responsibility for failure can be attributed to him without endangering the whole structure. It is significant, I think, that in all the explanations advanced, blame for the failure of the patient to recover was placed on human individuals. Where this is so the theory that the *vu* who punish infractions of the moral order by sending disease, are influenced by propiation or expiation, can continue to exist.

One interesting aspect of the subject of disease as a sanction in any given culture is the relation between sorcery and the sanction. We are familiar with societies in which a clear distinction is made between two fundamentally different types of causation, one traceable to human, the other to non-human action. In such cases it may be that sorcery is useful as a mechanism to relieve the sanction of a potentially dangerous amount of strain, in that it offers an alternative explanation for diseases which could not conveniently be attributed to moral infractions. However, as is well

---

[5] As the Government was involved in this case, this was not possible.

[6] It may be remembered that when Lemeki did not recover after the first *i mandrali*, the same *vuniwai* was not consulted for the second attempt. Unfortunately I neglected to make inquiries concerning this point but it may well have been that Lemeki's failure to regain his health was attributed to some fault of the *vuniwai* in this instance.

known, sorcery may itself function as a sanction, and the fear of sorcery act as a deterrent to anti-social behavior. On this basis there may be established a close relationship between sorcery and the religious sanction. Such, I believe, is the case in Fiji.

So far in this discussion of disease as a sanction we have been considering only those diseases classified as *mate ni vanua*, the native category comprising diseases due to the anger of the *vu*. It has previously been mentioned that considerable confusion exists in regard to the classification of diseases attributed to sorcery. According to some informants diseases of this type were not to be placed in one category with *mate ni vanua*; while others grouped the two types together. There was however unanimity of opinion regarding the distinct line of separation between, on the one side, *mate vayaŋo*, and on the other *mate ni vanua* and diseases resulting from sorcery. Since only two categories are named, the tendency of certain informants to group together the diseases attributed to sorcery and the *mate ni vanua*, is quite understandable. And, as I have already mentioned certain other facts would appear to support this classification: in the performance of sorcery a definite role is assigned to the *vu* so that witchcraft is not exclusively a human affair; likewise in the matter of therapeutic treatment, there is no distinction between *mate ni vanua* and diseases resulting from sorcery. Furthermore, when we consider disease in its function as a sanction it becomes apparent that diseases attributed to sorcery might well be grouped with the *mate ni vanua* on the grounds that both are ultimately regarded as due to infractions of the social order. In fact, the case material shows that the same type of anti-social behavior which in one instance might be punished by the *vu*, would in another, occasion the practice of sorcery. Consequently sorcery appears, in Fijian society, to be one aspect of the disease sanction.

Bibliography

Brewster, A. B.:
(1) *Circumcision in Noikoro, Noemala, Mboumbutho (Fiji)*. Journal of the Royal Anthropological Institute of Great Britain and Ireland, vol. 49, 1919.
(2) *The Hill Tribes of Fiji*. Philadelphia, 1922.

Clements, F. E.:
(1) *Primitive Concepts of Disease*. University of California Publications in American Archaeology and Ethnology. vol. 32, no. 2, 1932.

Corney, B. S.:
(1) *Certain Mutilations Practiced by the Natives of the Viti Islands*. Australasian Association for the Advancement of Science. Vol. 2, 1890.
(2) *Leprosy Stones in Fiji*. Folklore, vol. 7, 1896.

Deane, W.:
(1) *Fijian Society*. London, 1921.

Fison, L.:
(1) *The Nanga or Sacred Stone Inclosure of Wainimala, Fiji*. Journal of the Royal Anthropological Institute of Great Britain and Ireland. vol. 14, 1884–85.
(2) *Selections from the Letters of Fison and Howitt to Lewis H. Morgan*. Ed. by B. J. Stern. American Anthropologist, vol. 32, 1930.

Fortune, Reo:
(1) *Manus Religion*. Memoirs of the American Philosophical Society. vol. 3, 1935.

Hazlewood, David:
(1) *A Fijian and English Dictionary*. London, 1850.

Hocart, A. M.:
(1) *On the Meaning of Kalou and the Origin of Fijian Temples*. Journal of the Royal Anthropological Institute of Great Britain and Ireland. vol. 42, 1912.
(2) *On the Meaning of the Fijian Word Turanga*. Man, vol. 13, 1913.
(3) *Notes on Fijian Totemism*. Anthropos, Vol. 9, 1914.
(4) *Lau Islands, Fiji*. Bishop Museum Bulletin, no. 62, Honolulu, 1929.
(5) *Alternate Generations in Fiji*. Man, vol. 31, 1931.

Joske, A. B.:
(1) *The Nanga of Viti Levu*. Internationales Archiv für Ethnologie. Vol. 2, 1888.

De Marzan, P. J.:
(1) *Le Totemisme aux Iles Fiji*. Anthropos, vol. 2, 1907.
(2) *Sur Quelques Sociétés Secrètes aux Iles Fiji*. Anthropos, vol. 3, 1908.
(3) *Le Culte des Mortes aux Fiji, Grande-île Interieure*. Anthropos, vol. 4, 1909.

Myres, C. S.:
(1) *Disease and Medicine*. Article in Hasting's Encyclopedia of Religion and Ethics.

Pettazzoni, R.:
(1) *La Confession des Péchés*. Trans. by R. Monnot. Paris, 1931.

Rivers, W. H. R.:
(1) *Totemism in Fiji*. Man, vol. 8, 1908.
(2) *History of Melanesian Society*. Cambridge, 1914.
(3) *Medicine, Magic and Religion*. London, 1924.

ROUGIER, P. E.:

(1) *Maladies et Medicines à Fiji Autrefois et Aujourd'hui*. Anthropos, vol. 2, 1907.

SEEMANN, BERTHOLD: Flora Vitiensis. London, 1865–73.

SPENCER, D. M.:

(1) *Fijian Dreams and Visions*. Twenty-fifth Anniversary Studies of the Philadelphia Anthropological Society. Philadelphia, 1937.

THOMSON, BASIL:

(1) *Article on Ancestor Worship*, in Hasting's Encyclopedia of Religion and Ethics.

(2) *The Fijians*. A Study in the Decay of Custom. London, 1908.

WILLIAMS, T. AND CALVERT, J.:

(1) *Fiji and the Fijians*. New York, 1859.

WEBB, A. J.:

(1) *Observations on the Hill Tribes of Navitilevu*. Australasian Association for the Advancement of Science. Vol. 2, 1890.

GLOSSARY

i mandrali, propitiatory offering consisting of food and *yangona*.

i ndrotci, substances used in witchcraft; witchcraft.

i soro, offering made to obtain pardon for offenses committed against the living.

i taukei, owner, especially those members of the clan which owns the village, as distinguished from "foreign" inhabitants of the village.

i thavu, object or objects associated with the clan.

lewa nitu, female spirits.

luveniwai, name of a certain class of spirits; also name of a cult which centered around these spirits.

ma iti, a feast, consisting always of ya gona and food.

masi, barkcloth.

masumasu, prayer.

mata gali, the patrilineal clan organization.

mate, sickness; death.

mate ni vanua, "sickness of the land", i.e. disease caused by spirits.

mate vaya o, "disease of the body", i.e. disease resulting from incidental circumstances.

mbito, subdivision of the clan; house belonging to the subdivision.

mburua, final funeral ceremony.

ndau ndrondrotci, sorceror, anyone who practices witchcraft.

ni tu, generic term for spirit.

tambua, whale's tooth.

tolayandra, one who sees visions, a seer.

tuwawa, name of a class of spirits.

vu, source, origin, cause; spirits which have never been human; especially ancestral spirits of clans.

vuniwai, expert in Fijian therapy who cures disease by the aid of his spirit-helpers.

yalo, spirit, soul.

yalo mate, spirit of the dead.

yandra, vision.

yangona, the Fijian word for the *Piper methysticum*.

79

Appendix

Many of the diseases with which present day Fijians are afflicted have been introduced into the islands by Europeans and were unknown in aboriginal times. Leprosy, filariasis, yaws, ankylostomiasis, were endemic; there is some doubt as to the former existence of tuberculosis in Fiji; but measles, influenza, whooping cough, chicken pox, cholera, plague, small pox and venereal diseases have resulted from European contact. Dysentery is thought to have been introduced about 1803 by shipwrecked sailors. About 1875 a few natives of Fiji visited Australia and in returning brought with them measles;[1] 40,000 individuals out of an estimated population of 150,000 died, and 30 years later another epidemic occurred. Influenza was responsible for the death of 50% of the population in 1918.[2]

With regard to the present incidence of disease in relation to the pharmacological remedies which I have tabulated, some figures given in the Annual Medical and Health Report for the year 1934[3] are of interest. Of the general systematic and preventable diseases causing admission to hospitals in the colony during 1934, 14.77% were generative diseases, 11.70% digestive diseases, 6.19%, skin diseases, 3% eye diseases; injuries account for 14.40%, respiratory diseases for 5.53%, and urinary, nervous, cellular diseases, etc. for the rest. Of infective diseases, 55.50% were cases of influenza, 18.05%, cases of dysentery, 13.72%, cases of tuberculosis, 10.45% cases of yaws, etc. It will be seen from the table which I have prepared that diseases of the gastro-intestinal tract receive a great deal of attention, which is to be expected from the hospital figures; the number of remedies for diseases of the generative organs is also large. Although the number of remedies for skin diseases which I secured is somewhat out of proportion compared to the percentage of such diseases causing admission to the hospitals, this can be understood from the fact that the Fijians would not except in advanced cases, visit a hospital for treatment for skin diseases which are taken more or less as a matter of course. I must confess that I was startled, on surveying my material to discover

---

[1] The "prime reason for the outbreak in the West and the cause of Sir Arthur Gordon's 'Little War'. There the people ascribed the new mysterious malady to the wrath of the ancestral gods." Measles was this mysterious malady, see Brewster (2) p. 67.

[2] See The Colony of Fiji, 1874–1929. Suva 1929. p. 46 et. seq.

[3] Council paper no. 29, Suva 1935.

that I had not obtained a single remedy for ringworm, which is an extremely common disease, especially among the small children. It is probable, I think that there are native remedies for this disease, and that I failed through regrettable oversight on my part to secure them. However, as is stated in the Medical Report,[4] "The Pacific Islander is very apathetic about this skin condition, especially as it causes no morbidity or incapacity", and it is possible that this lack of concern is responsible for the failure of my native informants to bring me herbal remedies for ringworm. At the present time through the work of the anti-ringworm campaign which has been conducted by the Rockefeller Foundation, the Fijians are very much aware of the value of iodine in curing ringworm and I was frequently requested to paint the skins of children thus infected. It may be mentioned in this connection that in spite of the numerous remedies available for scabies, and the prevalence of this condition, I never saw anyone attempting to make use of the remedies.

Since the percentage of cases of tuberculosis causing admission to the hospitals is so high (according to medical opinion pulmonary tuberculosis is the "greatest direct cause of mortality among the native races today." Medical report. p. 4.) it is surprising to find that there are relatively few remedies in the table for diseases of the respiratory system.

The relatively high number of remedies for eye diseases is to be compared with the fact that of general systematic and preventable diseases causing admission to the hospitals 3% were eye diseases. In this connection it is of interest to note that 1% of the population of Tholo West is blind, according to the reports of the last census, which was taken in 1936.[5]

Generally speaking the hill people of Namataku at any rate do not take kindly to European medicines; they have retained considerable faith in their own therapeutic practices and herbal remedies. One old man with a very bad infection in his leg called in the district doctor, trained in European medical practices, who applied various remedies without any success; when his back was turned the patient summoned the native *vuniwai* (see p. 59 for details of the case) under whose care the infection was healed. The old man took pains to point out to me the fact that native remedies prevailed where European medicine was powerless. After the use of aspirin for headaches had been demonstrated somewhat spectacularly my supply of aspirin was rapidly exhausted but among the older people there were many who could not be persuaded to try it. My fre-

---

[4] *Op. cit.* p. 3.
[5] A Report on the 1936 Census, Suva 1936. p. 14.

quent offers to apply iodine to cuts and scratches usually met with a firm refusal.

A few general facts regarding native herbal remedies emerge from the table: Most frequently it is the leaf which is used and green leaves, only rarely dry ones are specified; root and bark are required in only a few instances. In most of the preparations for which water is needed, cold water is used. The epidermis which surrounds the lower part of the coconut leaf serves as a strainer and a length of bamboo is used as a container if a quantity of the medicine is made at one time.